Learning care lessons

the Tufnell Press,

London,
United Kingdom

www.tufnellpress.co.uk

email contact@tufnellpress.co.uk

British Library Cataloguing-in-Publication Data
A catalogue record for this book is
available from the British Library

paperback ISBN	*1872767 982*
ISBN-13	*978-1-872767-98-7*
Kindle	*978-1-872767-04-8*

Cover design by Nessa Finnegan

Printed in England and U.S.A. by Lightning Source

Learning care lessons:
Literacy, love, care and solidarity

by
Maggie Feeley

Ethnography and Education

The *Ethnography and Education* book series aims to publish a range of authored and edited collections including both substantive research projects and methodological texts and in particular we hope to include recent PhDs· Our priority is for ethnographies that prioritise the experiences and perspectives of those involved and that also reflect a sociological perspective with international significance· We are particularly interested in those ethnographies that explicate and challenge the effects of educational policies and practices and interrogate and develop theories about educational structures· policies and experiences· We value ethnographic methodology that involves long-term engagement with those studied in order to understand their cultures· that use multiple methods of generating data and that recognise the centrality of the researcher in the research process·

www·ethnographyandeducation·org

The editors welcome substantive proposals that seek to:

explicate and challenge the effects of educational policies and practices and interrogate and develop theories about educational structures, policies and experiences,

highlight the agency of educational actors,

provide accounts of how the everyday practices of those engaged in education are instrumental in social reproduction.

The editors are

Professor Dennis Beach, University College of Borås· Sweden,
Professor Sofia Marques da Silva, Porto University, Portuagal,
Professor Geoff Troman, Roehampton University, London and
Professor Geoffrey Walford, University of Oxford.

Contents

For
Survivors of abuses and their courageous mending

Acknowledgements

Many people have helped to shape this project and supported me in a host of indispensable ways. Some of those who gave me most assistance in this research cannot be named. For that reason, in naming no one, my wish is to thank everyone equally for the care-full support without which this work would have been a more lonely and difficult process.

The written document (especially any errors) has been my responsibility, but it has been formed and changed by insightful comments from research participants, loving family and friends, and peers in Equality Studies, University College Dublin. An avid proponent of care recognition supervised my original doctoral study. She steadily steered me with foresight and conviction and I am appreciative both of her inspirational intellect and her humanity. I am grateful to all who took the time to read my work, at various stages of development, and to affirm or challenge me in my thinking.

The wider research project has benefited from a range of sustaining relationships that nourished me bodily, emotionally and intellectually. I am indebted to the learners and literacy workers who welcomed me into a new part of the country and helped me to settle and find a location for this research. In particular, the survivors of institutional abuse accepted me into their community where I experienced the abundance of warmth and respect that they hold so preciously in their adult lives. I recognise that they opened up painful memories to me and I am truly thankful for all that they have taught me. I have come to share their dismay at the persistent lack of recognition of the abuses done to them, especially in the field of education.

This project has affirmed for me the gifts that care and literacy are in our lives and I acknowledge all the love, large and small, that has held me up in this work, and that goes on and on.

Foreword

Why Learning Care matters

Kathleen Lynch

What is significant about *Learning Care* is that it changes the way in which we discuss issues of equality in education; it highlights the role of the affective domains of life for learning and for education. In so doing, it extends the debate about equality in education from questions of (re) distributive justice (who gets access to what in education) and questions of respect (issues of identity recognition) to questions about relational justice. It highlights the issues raised by care ethicists about the importance of marrying an ethic of care to an ethic of justice when analysing equality in education. In so doing it does not deny the importance of class, gender, race, ethnicity and differences in ability in determining 'educational success'. Rather, it adds new questions about how care identities impact on learning, including care within the context of education and schooling.

Most people in Western societies spend about fourteen years in schools, which is between one sixth and one fifth of their entire life. Schooling is part of life, not just a preparation for life. Education in school plays a defining role in framing peoples' public identities as workers and learners. It matters in and of itself regardless of its future value.

The Latin root of the word education, 'educare', means 'to nurture' and develop. Education is formative: it is literally about making people what they are. Yet contemporary educational thinking continues to draw heavily from Cartesian thinking, emphasising the development of narrowly defined cognitive skills, especially logical mathematical intelligence and abstract reasoning (Gardner, 1983). Even the growing recognition of emotional and personal intelligence within developmental psychology has not unsettled the focus of education on the development of the educated person as one who services the economy. Moreover, the impact of Cartesian rationalism is intensifying with the glorification of performativity increasingly measured by league tables and rankings like the Programme for International Student Assessment (PISA) which are based or a narrow set of linguistic, mathematical and scientific skills. Thus, despite

... *'twentieth-century moves towards egalitarianism in education, the selection and segregation of those regarded as being gifted, talented, or of higher ability in better resourced schools and programmes is now increasingly acceptable ... The corollary to this is a more intense struggle by expanded middle classes to gain competitive advantages in education and in the global job market, accompanied by an increase in economic, social and racial inequalities for the losers in the competition.'* (Tomlinson, 2008: 59-60)

The focus on education for competitive advantage has led to a growing lack of attention to the need for care within the educational process as a value in itself (Noddings, 2005). Children in schools are defined increasingly in terms of their future market potential. At the individual level, the purpose of education is defined in terms of personalised human capital acquisition, making oneself skilled for the economy. *'The individual is expected to develop a productive and entrepreneurial relationship towards oneself* (Masschelein and Simons, 2002: 594). At the political level, both the Lisbon agreement and Europe 2020 focus on preparing citizens for the 'knowledge economy': knowledge is reduced to the status of an adjective in the service of the economy.

Love and care are the assumed foods on the table of emotional life for most people who have access to good primary caring: care is taken as a given, a good to which everyone has access. But as Maggie Feeley's research shows, this is not the case and care can be absence not only in the primary care domains of family settings, but also in secondary care contexts such as schools. Teachers are important players in a person's care life and how they care matters in terms of how and if people learn. If the focus on education is on performance, measured increasingly by limited indicators, and teachers are tested through their children's performance measurement on a narrow range of cognitive skills, then care is peripheralised. There is little incentive for educators to attend to care needs of those who are unable to learn when such care will not appear on a performance indicator.

Many children who attend schools have overwhelming needs that prevent them from learning. They may lack safety and security, food, love or care, or they may be subjected to violence and abuse. Even those children who are not at the negative extremes of the care spectrum can and do have crises in their lives when learning is secondary. In these situations, children's energies are devoted to managing their fears and anxieties; they are not devoted to learning.

Learning Care raises vital questions for educators about the role of care in learning. It shows that children's preoccupations are different to what adult educators often perceive them to be (Dodson, and Luttrell, 2011; Luttrell, 2013). As one of Maggie's contributors noted: *It would be very hard to learn if you feel that nobody cares about you. You are bound to build that wall and make sure that nobody gets in... I blocked people out and didn't want to have anyone coming near me because I had never had someone caring about me.* (Liam). Her research shows that children simply cannot learn if they do not feel.

Children and young people can and do define themselves through their relational lives (ibid) and these must be taken account of in the context of education. Equality-relevant differences between children are therefore, not only those of class, race, ethnicity, gender or ability, though these remain important. Children are affective relational beings for whom love and care are of paramount importance, both within and outside school. While affective inequalities intersect with other inequalities, Maggie's research shows that they have a discrete and significant impact on learning in their own right.

Kathleen Lynch
Professor of Equality Studies
Head of School of Social Justice
University College Dublin

References

Dodson, L. and Luttrell, W. (2011) Families Facing Untenable Choices, *Contexts,* 10 (1): 38-42.

Luttrell, W. (2012) Making Boys' Care Worlds Visible, *THYMOS: Journal of Boyhood Studies,* 6 (2): 186-202.

Masschelein, J. and Simons, M. (2002) An adequate education in a globalised world? A note on immunisation against being-together, *Journal of Philosophy of Education,* 36 (4): 589-608.

Tomlinson, S. (2008) Gifted, Talented and High Ability: selection for education in a one-dimensional world, *Oxford Review of Education,* 34 (1): 59–74.

Introduction

Learning Care lessons

Learning means forgetting as well as remembering.

(Tom Bentley, 1998:187)

This book gives an account of an ethnographic study of the literacy learning experiences of survivors of abuse in Irish industrial schools. The process involved extensive memory work over a three-year period, watching, listening and conversing with adults about their childhood education in state care institutions. As well as memories recounted in the day-to-day setting of the Lighthouse adult community-learning centre, some early recollections of learning literacy were sparked in the adult literacy setting. As part of the Centre adult learning programme where I occasionally acted as a voluntary tutor, an echo of some very specific childhood experience of school might surface that prompted new areas of discussion. Over the period of my sustained presence in the community, significant evidence of the care that supports us as learners was uncovered and it is this affective continuum from love to abuse, and its role in formal and informal learning that is the particular focus of the study.

The idea of memory in the quotation above is salient in that what follows reveals how recollection of past childhood abuses continues to interrupt contemporary adult learning experiences. At the same time, in the 'dangerous memories' of learning recounted by survivors of institutional abuse the comfortable hegemonic accounts of 'care' are disturbed and there is growing solidarity in a reframed collective identity (Zaviršek, 2006). Memories are at once individual, collective and political and the challenging and hopeful dimensions of critical ethnographic memory work, as a form of praxis, are sometimes activated (Zembylas and Bekerman, 2008: 127). Reflecting the Freirean process of conscientisation, reflection and action, the critical ethnographic process in the heightened context of intensive public debate, meant that many survivors of institutional abuse increasingly saw their educational neglect as both personal and political (Freire, 1972; 1973). This will be evident later in their analysis of the systemic nature of the injustices that were perpetrated against them.

As part of a wider public remembering of institutional abuses, this research articulated and highlighted educational neglect that was often overshadowed by more shocking detail of corporal and sexual abuses. Survivors were adamant that their ongoing educational disadvantage merited greater recognition. As a critical educational ethnography the study involved not only several years of exploration within the community setting but also a conscious desire to contribute to the exposure of systematic social disadvantage that caused, and continues to cause and reproduce, educational inequalities. As Thomas (1993: 9), cited in O'Reilly (2009: 53) describes:

> Critical ethnography takes seemingly mundane events, even repulsive ones and reproduces them in a way that exposes broader social processes of control, taming, power imbalance, and the symbolic mechanisms that impose one set of preferred meanings or behaviours over others.

The study began with the assumption that in educational terms, being excluded from literacy use is a gross inequality that effects not only individuals but also generations of families and communities. Literacy 'difficulties' occur in the context of wider economic, political and socio-cultural injustice and amount to a form of state care-lessness, although individuals, families and communities are often held to blame. Through the extreme context of institutional abuse, I want to magnify the role of affective aspects of in/equality in relation to learning literacy and to highlight the enduring impacts of a care deficit on immediate and future learning identities. The memories and voices of survivors of institutional abuse in Irish industrial schools are at the core of the text and the themes of literacy, inequality and care that they illuminate are universal and timeless.

Industrial schools

Industrial schools were first established in Scotland, operated throughout Britain under the 1857 Industrial Schools Act and were extended to Ireland in 1868. The schools were intended as a complement, and subsequently an alternative to the Reformatory School system. They had a remit to provide state care, education and vocational preparation for poor children whose family life was deemed no longer viable. It was thought that exposure to meaningful 'industry' would save young people at risk of following their adult family members into lives perceived as being of social, religious and moral deviation.

In Ireland, the industrial schools were part of a wider portfolio of institutional provision that included Mother and Baby homes, County Homes for the destitute and the infamous Magdalene Laundries. The latter forced many, including some mothers of those in industrial schools, into unpaid labour in profitable laundries run by religious orders. The exposure of their harsh realities has been the focus of a recent Irish State apology (in 2013) and a plan to compensate the Magdalene women who are still alive today.

The institutional care system reflected and reproduced the class order of the day. Despite often being conflated, state-funded industrial schools were separate from privately funded orphanages, which catered for middle-class and upper middle-class children of the time. Orphanages were often run by the same religious orders as industrial schools but in a notably less punishing manner.

While the Catholic Church used the operation of industrial schools, and other institutions, to maintain strict religious, cultural and ethnic control, state structures ultimately enabled the system through the letter and practice of the law, the allocation of maintenance grants and the regulatory role of the Department of Education (Raftery and O'Sullivan, 1999). To this day, the uncoupling of the alliance between church and state, particularly in the Irish education system, is a live debate that has yet to reach a conclusive outcome.

Industrial schools were not a solely Irish phenomenon. Reports of comparable abusive systems of child-detention, directed and operated by Catholic religious orders during the nineteenth and twentieth centuries, have also surfaced in Scotland, Australia, the USA and Canada. The same Irish Christian Brothers and various female religious orders such as the Sisters of Mercy that are subjects in the data in this book, have been implicated in the histories of abuse emerging across many continents.

At the time of the creation of an independent Irish State in the 1920s, Britain was already moving away from the institutionalised, industrial school model in favour of more child-friendly approaches to primary care. In Ireland, although they were known to be exceptionally punitive, the schools were allowed to operate virtually without either challenge or sanction for over one hundred years. In 1970, the Kennedy Report (Government of Ireland, 1970) was highly critical of the system and the decades that followed saw survivors speaking out about their experiences so that the extent of their multiple abuses became increasingly public. In 1999, the State apologised to survivors, instigated a compensatory redress system and established an education fund for survivors and their families.

In his apology on behalf of the State to survivors of abuse in Irish industrial schools, the Taoiseach (Irish Prime Minister) highlighted the importance of love and care in the lives of children and the detrimental impact of a loveless and careless childhood on later adult lives.

On behalf of the State and all its citizens, the government wishes to make a sincere and long overdue apology to the victims of childhood abuse for our collective failure to intervene, to detect their pain, to come to their rescue... .all children need love and security. Too many of our children were denied this love, care and security. Abuse ruined their childhoods and has been an ever present part of their adult lives reminding them of a time when they were helpless. I want to say to them that we believe that they were gravely wronged, and that we must do all we can now to overcome the lasting effects of their ordeals.

(*An Taoiseach Bertie Ahern, 11 May 1999 as cited in Health Board Executive (HBE), 2002*).

The physical, sexual and emotional abuses of children in industrial schools have understandably overshadowed the detail of the educational neglect that accompanied those atrocities. Nevertheless, survivors feel passionately about the lost opportunities that resulted from the paucity of their learning experiences and make a direct connection between reclaiming some of that learning opportunity and the long process of healing.

The ambiguity of 'care'

Throughout this work 'care' has emerged as an ambiguous term that simultaneously suggests both positive and negative experiences in the affective domain. Spending time 'in care' was a shameful, stigmatised and often hidden factor in people's later lives and connoted none of the relational benefits of being part of a loving and supportive bond. Survivors of institutional abuse in industrial schools rarely felt either cared for or cared about by those in the institutions and so the term 'care' is often met with understandable cynicism. Despite the ambiguities about care, I have persevered with the word in the hope that in association with 'learning', 'care' can be reclaimed, as a concept that describes all that is best in learning relationships.

Literacy and care

The quest to describe what I have named *learning care*, with those whose childhood was spent in industrial schools, is set in the context of adult literacy where the vast majority of learners have a lot of forgetting to do. They often need to move beyond their harmful memories and emotions associated with formal schooling, before they can start learning in adulthood. Most adult literacy narratives include unhappy accounts of lost opportunities, care-lessness and failure to facilitate the development of human potential. In relation to unmet literacy needs[1], the participants in this research clearly highlight extreme, intricately interwoven inequalities including pivotal neglect in the affective domain. So, learning literacy is one part of the story and inequality of care is another and each element and its place in the study merits clarification at this early stage.

Literacy and me—an equality issue

After thirty years' work as a literacy tutor, organiser and manager, the conceptual framework of equality, developed in Equality Studies, University College Dublin brought a fresh perspective to my work.[2] The interdisciplinary framework illustrates how degrees of inequality of resources, power, respect and recognition and care interconnect to create and sustain disadvantage for individuals and groups in many dimensions of life (Baker *et al.*, 2004). Drawing from a number of fields including economics, political theory, education, sociology and law the framework adopts a multidisciplinary position in order to address the complex nature of inequality. The underpinning theory identifies 'equality of condition' as the ultimate objective of those who aspire to create a more socially just world (Baker *et al.*, 2004: 33-42; Lynch and Baker, 2005). This is the most radical form of equality and the only lasting way to change unequal social systems. An exposure to a multidimensional view of social injustice got me thinking about literacy from an egalitarian perspective and enabled me to link my knowledge and experience of literacy education with egalitarian theory (Feeley, 2005; 2007; 2010).

In particular, the salience of the affective domain of equality struck a chord with my own literacy work. In some ways it was stating the obvious to describe the learning of literacy as an affective concern. Nevertheless, as in wider society, care is a vital, often gendered and voluntary, but largely invisible component of adult literacy. As I reached the end of this study, a number of literacy students with whom I had previously worked, came back to my mind. There was the young man, Jack, who was referred to me in the 1980s by a psychiatrist because he had severed his index finger at the second joint. Jack explained that he was fed up inventing excuses for why he could not fill forms and satisfy other public

1. I use the term 'unmet literacy needs' to avoid the implication of individual deficit in phrases like people with literacy difficulties, essential skills deficits ... and so on.
2. The equality framework will be described in detail in chapter two.

demands on literacy. Now he need only show his finger and the demand was withdrawn without him suffering any further indignity. What was fascinating was that he was left-handed and had damaged his right hand so that he always had the option to learn literacy at a later date. He subsequently told me about his childhood in institutional care that had resonance with the findings in this study.

I also remembered a literacy group in West Belfast where it emerged over time that five out of the eight adults that I worked with had been sexually abused, as children, in their own community. Yet again there was the narrative of a man in a rural border town who had been brutally beaten by a teacher who favoured the children of the wealthier people in the town and vented his frustrations on those who were powerless. All these and a host of other adult learners had been talking about care inequalities all along and I had not the consciousness of affective equality to hear them accurately.

Generally, such lack of recognition has meant that the care associated with learning literacy (and other things) remains neglected both in theory, research and to some extent, in practice. In turn, this has led to an affective void in literacy policy considerations, resourcing and practitioner training. So, this empirical study sought to explore the links between care and literacy with a view to increasing the capacity and reach of those who work to meaningfully address persistent levels of unmet literacy needs.[3]

Caring about profit before people

Literacy has increasingly become a matter of corporate concern for business and Lankshear and Knobel (2003) suggest that it is this, rather than care for the educationally disadvantaged that accounts for growing focus on adult literacy in the past few decades. As far back as 1992 it was estimated that $40 billion was lost annually to US business because of people with unmet literacy needs (Organisation for Economic Co-operation and Development, (OECD) 1992). At the same time, the Centre for Educational Research and Innovation report (1992) argued that fifty per cent production development in the US economy

3. An estimated 500,000 adults in Ireland have not been given access to functional literacy and only eleven per cent of them are involved in adult learning (National Adult Literacy Agency, 2011). Currently, over thirty per cent of children in disadvantaged Irish primary schools have not acquired the literacy level needed to cope with transition to secondary education (Department of Education and Science, 2005). Similar numbers of adults in other countries with universal primary and secondary education have unmet literacy needs. The data about other countries will be discussed in chapter two.

could be attributed to on-the-job training and learning. This was twice as important a contribution as that made by new technologies at the time and began a trend of workplace learning and measuring gains from increases in human capital. The Centre for Educational Research and Innovation (CERI) report also led directly to the International Adult Literacy Studies throughout the 1990s and prompted some to argue that the *crisis* of the literacy gap was not so much a fall in educational standards as a rise in demands on literacy in modern economies, primarily out of a concern for profits (Hamilton and Barton, 2000; Lankshear and Knobel, 2003). Such critique of dominant, positivist understandings has done much to problematise literacy and spark debate in the field (Brandt and Clinton 2002; Kim, 2003; Reder and Davila 2005; Street, 2003). Nevertheless, although the ideological and socially situated nature of literacy is now more widely accepted, the equally important location of literacy in the affective domain is largely ignored.

Learning care

The impetus for the research was a desire to shed new light on persistent, intransigent levels of unmet literacy needs and to increase our knowledge of the intricate role that care (both in attitude and action) plays in supporting learning. Hence, the text explores how a focus on affective aspects of equality, making a robust form of pedagogical care central in our work, may help refine our understanding of adult literacy learning practices so that the generational cycle of unmet literacy needs can be broken. Working from an egalitarian perspective, these twin threads of literacy and care are woven throughout the study.

Both literacy and care are important considerations in the research. As a pivotal area of childhood and adult education, literacy is recognised as a site of major learning inequalities. Literacy provides the backdrop for the study of affective aspects of learning and as such is explored in the literature and the empirical data. Nevertheless, in terms of providing a new perspective on literacy inequalities, care figures as the primary research focus with the hope of producing a model of literacy *learning care* that could then be applied to more diverse learning contexts.

I should say from the beginning that 'learning care' is not some kind of nebulous good intent but rather a skilful, respectful, empowering approach to facilitating learning. At the outset, *learning care* was understood to mean the attitudes and the actions, both paid and unpaid, that support individuals and groups on their learning journey. The core purpose of the research was to further explore the experiences of learning care of a specific group and in the context of learning literacy and thereby to define learning care a little more clearly.

I coined the term *learning care* to capture the idea that affective aspects of learning are not incidental but rather a central and consistent element of the learning process. This is the case even when the degree of learning care is at the extreme, negative end of the care continuum and expressed as harm.

Some aspects of care and emotion in education have been well-researched and written about and are discussed below. This study looks at care in the learning of literacy, both in childhood and adulthood, from the perspective of the learner rather than the educator. In this, it is novel both to the field of literacy and care. In the case of research about institutional abuse, the study highlights the often overshadowed area of educational neglect that has a lifelong impact on those for whom childhood was care-less.

Why 'learning care' matters

Despite continued state complacency about the provision of all aspects of care in wider society, others have illustrated that care is an inescapable feature of our lives (Baker *et al.* 2004; 2009; Engster, 2005; Fineman, 2004; Gheaus, 2009; Lynch and McLaughlin, 1995; Nussbaum, 2000; 2001). We are interdependent but not always relationally adept and so we need to be more conscious of developing an ethos of care in interpersonal encounters of all kinds (Baker *et al.*, 2004; Engster, 2005; Nussbaum, 2001). The availability and quality of care in every aspect of our lives has much significance in terms of our ongoing development and self-actualisation both individually and collectively. This suggests that we need to learn about care and how to be more proficient at care giving and receiving. The universality of care also means that to be fair, care responsibilities and care work need to be equally shared and the benefits equally experienced. In reality, care slips under the radar and that allows affective injustices to persist virtually unnoticed or unchallenged.

As well as its pleasures and rewards, care has gendered, burdensome and costly aspects to it that are often disregarded but that nonetheless require recognition and resourcing (Darmanin, 2003; Fineman, 2004; Kittay, 2002; Lynch, 2007). This is true also of the care that supports learning where complex inequalities operate to determine the extent to which individuals and groups are enabled to reap the benefits of educational provision. Maeve O'Brien has analysed the way in which mothers' capacity to support children's learning and overall educational well-being is influenced by a complex range of factors. She maps the mix of economic, social, cultural and emotional resources demanded of mothers in the support of their children's education and describes how disparities in these resources contribute in turn to persistent educational inequalities (O'Brien, 2005). Others have focused on care and the school curriculum (Cohen, 2006; McClave, 2005); teachers' emotional labour (Hargreaves, 2000; 2001); the role of the affective domain in educational ideology (Lynch *et al.*, 2007) and the need for an explicit ethic of care in schools (Noddings, 1992; 2006; 2007). Building on the work of Noddings, Rebecca Powell (1999) suggested that a pedagogical ethic of care (what she called *agape*[4]) was needed if school literacy in pluralist societies was to be truly empowering and transformative. In the context of schooling in the US, Wendy Luttrell's photovoice studies with young people have shown how children are challenging dominant discourses about the importance of care in their lives (Luttrell, 2013).

> The children's counter-narratives suggest an alternative economy of value within school that reach beyond performance measures and test scores that have become the sole calculus of learning and success.
>
>   (Luttrell, 2013: forthcoming)

In this book, the affective focus takes a different turn towards the field of adult literacy. In particular, the perspective moves from the more widely considered role of the teacher or parent as caregiver, to focus on the learner as a care recipient in a learning relationship.

The location of the empirical study

The research design and methodology required careful consideration and lengthy preparation because both literacy and care are sensitive areas not readily opened up to outsiders. I explored a number of possible research sites and volunteered for a year as a literacy tutor with a range of youth and adult groups. I wanted to build relationships of trust and to observe and discuss the potential for empirical research in these different settings. It became clear that detailed reflection about their care and literacy biographies was inappropriate for a number of groups and individuals. Many were already limited in the time they could devote to literacy and participation in research was one time demand too many. Others had life stories that were too harrowing to pick over without risking further hurt and

4. *Agape* is the term used to denote Christian love as distinct from erotic love or simple affection. It has its origins in the Greek word agape connoting brotherly love.

damage. Despite their extremes of neglect, those who call themselves 'survivors of institutional abuse' were open to the opportunity to relate their experience, to be believed and to find healing in the process. 'Survivors of institutional abuse', was favoured as an alternative the term 'victims', by ex-residents of industrial schools who attended the Lighthouse Centre. A range of abuses had been reported by them including emotional, physical and sexual abuse. Neglect, including educational disadvantage was also recognised by the Residential Institutions Redress Act (2002) as a form of abuse eligible for compensation under 'loss of opportunity'. All those who attended the Lighthouse Centre experienced one or many forms of abuse and many were working to improve their level of literacy.

The final location for the study therefore emerged organically and the Lighthouse Centre for adult survivors of institutional abuse in industrial schools became the ethnographic research site. The Lighthouse Centre is a pseudonym for an adult education and advice centre established in Dublin by and for survivors of abuse in Irish industrial schools. The Centre provided a range of adult learning opportunities including literacy, anger management, art therapy and personal development. Advice was also available about family tracing, counselling, and legal matters. The Centre functioned as a community centre and at the time of the study was attended on an average day by eighty people.

Ethical issues

Access to the community was through an identified 'gatekeeper' with whom the ethnographic process was fully discussed and agreed. She in turn required me to be interviewed by the local literacy providers to establish that I was in a position to provide voluntary literacy support to community members. My presence in the community as a researcher was entirely transparent and all those who shared their memories with me were fully informed about the study and any possible future use of the data. They were assured of confidentiality, anonymity and their right to withdraw from the process at any time. Each aspect of the process was negotiated and indeed, on hearing their allocated pseudonym, some asked for it to be changed to something of their own choosing. For those who were called by a number rather than a name this aspect of the research process took on added significance. Because many participants had literacy issues, consent forms were read aloud and signed as a mutual agreement by both the researcher and the participants.

Findings and limitations

The findings of this study suggest that unequal literacy distribution is synonymous with intricate and interconnected inequalities. In the context of learning, facilitating literacy becomes care and a failure to do so is akin to abuse. Unequal literacy outcomes have therefore both a real and symbolic value in articulating individual experiences of care-related in/equalities. They also exemplify the failure of a state to care equally for and about the learning needs of all its citizens. In this sense, unmet literacy needs may be viewed as a form of state harm[5] that merits further attention from a zemiological perspective (Hillyard *et al.*, 2004).

The project described here is novel in the literacy context in that it has adopted a critical ethnographic and practitioner research paradigm. This has meant engaging with a specific community of interest—survivors of abuse in industrial schools—over a period of three years. A protracted investment of time was necessary to build enduring relationships of trust that would enable in-depth discussion of the dual stigma of institutional care and unmet literacy needs. A critical case sample was chosen so that the findings might hold relevance not only for the community of interest but also for other adult literacy contexts and learning in general (Patton, 1980; 1990).

The study makes a number of innovative contributions to our knowledge about both care in/equality and literacy. Literacy is redefined from an egalitarian perspective, building on the work of New Literacy Studies to expose the injustices in the social context where literacy occurs. Because this context is socially constructed, unmet literacy needs are therefore construed as a form of state harm. With the objective of carrying out a care-full inquiry, an emancipatory, ethnographic, practitioner research process was designed and deployed. Unless otherwise stated all the words quoted are those of survivors of institutional abuse and they form the backbone of the study.

Limitations are inevitable and I chose to concentrate on the experience of literacy learners and the extent to which their care biographies impacted on

5. The idea of studying social or state harm also known as Zemiology has been developed to draw attention to the way in which certain damaging acts become criminalised while others escape that judgement. This is even though their detrimental consequences can, like unmet literacy needs, be far reaching. Proponents of Zemiology suggest that harm may be physical, economic/financial, emotional and psychological and related to cultural safety. This perspective will be elaborated in chapter three.

their capacity to learn. In that sense this is unapologetically a one-sided view. Exploring learning care from the care-giver's perspective, and indeed beyond the field of literacy, was outside the scope of this study and is the work of another day. Despite these limitations, the overall goal was to extract a model of literacy learning care that will support the current literacy care-giver's role and this has been accomplished.

Outline of the book

Following on from this introduction, the book has seven chapters. chapter one outlines the organic process of exploring and developing an ethnographic literacy practitioner research study where the role of researcher overlaps with that of literacy facilitator and reciprocal learner. Learning relationships were both the focus of the study and key to all stages of the process and the rich, diverse care biographies of participants allowed for comparative as well as descriptive analysis. This was a lengthy and at times arduous research process with enormous ethical dimensions in relation to the vulnerabilities associated with both adult literacy and institutional care. An ethnographic approach allowed for a respectful, unhurried immersion in an adult learning community with vast expertise, albeit by omission, in the affective dimensions of learning. The participants' narratives were gripping and the level of analysis already carried out by survivors in relation to their experiences was extensive and shared with me with boundless generosity. chapter one describes an ethnography of care.

The second chapter sets the educational context for the study by exploring the different theoretical perceptions of literacy and locating these within an equality perspective. The changing nature of literacy and the way that unmet literacy needs function as a barometer for inequality is explored. Functional (Organisation for Economic Co-operation and Development), critical (Freirean) and cultural, socially situated understandings of literacy (New Literacy Studies) are outlined and their implications for egalitarian social change are considered. The conceptual framework of equality (Baker *et al.*, 2004; 2009) that underpins the whole study is introduced and the argument for an egalitarian theory of literacy is proposed.

Chapter three looks at why affective inequality matters. With a focus on the particular element of affective equality within the equality framework (Baker *et al.*, 2004; 2009) the possible interaction between literacy and care is explored. A 'dynamic cycle of care' is proposed that depicts learning care playing an important intermediary role between contexts of equality (economic, political, cultural, affective) and literacy learning. This chapter illustrates the neglected agency of love, care and solidarity in literacy learning and considers the concept of harm—the counter face of care. Borrowing from the field of criminology, the notion of adopting a social harm perspective is explored in the context of literacy (Hillyard *et al.*, 2004). Here, unmet literacy needs are associated with the negative end of the social care continuum and the implications of a state duty of care in relation to basic education are discussed.

There are three findings chapters. In the first of these—chapter four the interface between resources and literacy learning care are explored through the data. Resources are understood not just in terms of financial assets but also the whole portfolio of carer capitals that support literacy learning. Learning care is described as a form of labour that involves a range of temporal, physical, emotional, material and cultural resources. Inequalities in all these resources are shown to have impacted on the degrees of learning care available to individuals and their subsequent literacy outcomes.

Cultural aspects of learning and in particular status-related inequalities are examined in chapter five for the way that they impacted on learning care and literacy outcomes. They show that even within the harsh circumstances in the industrial school, further hierarchical divisions were created that influenced literacy learning. Ethnicity, disability status, class and other aspects of diversity were seen to create additional inequalities within an already disadvantaged community.

In the third findings chapter, chapter six, we turn our attention to literacy and the affective/power interface. Both state and institutional power were significant determining factors in the lives of survivors of abuse in industrial schools. The degree to which power was affectively distributed and enacted in the institution, and in particular in the classroom, was crucially important in whether literacy was acquired or not. The data articulately describe the lived experience of power-related care inequalities and their relationship to the learning of literacy. Here care is most starkly illustrated through its absence.

The findings about learning care are summarised and discussed in chapter seven both in relation to the immediate research context and the wider contemporary literacy sector. A model of learning care is elaborated. The findings suggest that four strands of learning care are significant in learning literacy: primary learning care in the home, secondary learning care at school, tertiary learning care with peers and a fundamental, underwriting state duty of care.

The implications of each form of learning care is explored in relation to the field of literacy today and hopefully these interwoven strands of care will help point to the transformational potential of recognising the affective dimension in all literacy work. However, it is worth noting that it is in the state duty of care that the weakest and most damaging link emerges.

State responsibilities

The impetus for this study came from over twenty-five years' experience as a practitioner and a manager of adult literacy provision in Northern Ireland. This community-based educational work coincided with the most intense period of political dysfunction and violent conflict and I became familiar with the stark and complex lived realities of those at society's margins, in the hardest of times. It was in these misrecognised, disrespected groups that unmet literacy needs were then, and continue now to be located. My experience led me to view literacy inequalities as, both literally and symbolically, an expression of state-sanctioned, if not state-constructed social injustice. At the same time, a persistent, deficit discourse constantly held educationally disadvantaged people responsible for their own unequal life outcomes. For a literacy practitioner who knew this to be untrue, it was an increasingly frustrating and unhopeful context in which to work. I wanted to have more effective arguments that accurately and authentically identified the structural genesis and reproduction of educational and wider social disadvantage. My hope is that this book relocates primary responsibility for learning inequalities in the failure of the state to honour its own part in relation to a duty of care.

Chapter 1

An ethnography of care

> Lack of respect, though less aggressive than an outright insult, can take an equally wounding form. No Insult is offered another person, but neither is recognition extended; he or she is not seen—as a full human being whose presence matters.   (Richard Sennett, 2003: 4)

Introduction

When a series of disappointing policy responses followed the Organisation for Economic and Cultural Development's literacy studies of the late 1990s, the hopes of adult educators, that our day had come, gradually evaporated (Department of Education for Northern Ireland, 1998; Moser, 1999). In 2000, I took a year off work to do an M.Sc. in Equality Studies. This time for reflection convinced me that literacy would be more powerfully and meaningfully defined in terms of issues of equality. I was particularly interested by the exploration of affective inequality that had become a new focus of research in Equality Studies (Baker *et al.*, 2004; Lynch, 1989; Lynch and McLaughlin, 1995). Care inequalities had often emerged in the narratives of literacy learners and yet this entire aspect of literacy disadvantage remained unstudied. So, I conceived the notion of exploring the relationship between literacy and affective aspects of inequality and took early retirement from my position as Head of Department of Adult and Community Education in a Northern Ireland College to pursue this research project. My motivation was therefore not investment in an academic career but rather, at the end of decades of adult literacy work, to explore the concept of learning care with adult learners and hopefully shed light on persistent educational inequalities.

The research context that is the focus here (2004-2007) was therefore, that of heightened adult literacy activity that followed the international studies of the 1990s (OECD, 1995; 1996; 1997; 1998). The most influential was the International Adult Literacy Survey (IALS) (OECD, 1998). Despite the failure to problematise the meaning of literacy in adult lives and their predominantly economic motivation (Hamilton and Barton, 2000), these studies did increase both awareness and funding of this marginalised corner of the education field.

The subsequent strategising and target setting exposed the inequalities within the funding process and the persistent reluctance of adults with unmet literacy needs to participate in learning. The issue of non-participation often forms part of a literacy deficit discourse and one goal of this research is to expose state, rather than individual failure as a cause of unmet literacy needs. More than a decade since IALS the predominant interest in adult literacy remains clear. The Programme for the International Assessment of Adult Competencies (PIAAC) builds on the areas covered by IALS to include an additional focus on literacy in the workplace and problem solving in technology rich environments (OECD, 2010). The meaning of literacy has certainly expanded since the original IALS but whether levels of literacy justice have increased remains to be seen.

Despite increased rhetoric and some increased funding, adult literacy remains a relatively low educational priority. Although the fundamental importance of literacy for all other forms of learning and development has been widely accepted, vast inequalities in its distribution persist and compensatory actions are ineffective in stemming the tide of generational disadvantage. Research has shown that it is difficult to find evidence of reducing levels of literacy inequalities in UK, USA and Ireland, despite increased attention and funding (Archer and Weir, 2005; Sticht, 2000; Hamilton and Hillier; 2006). Unmet literacy needs continue to track wider disadvantage and it is clearly that fundamental issue that needs to be addressed for lasting resolutions to occur (Wilkinson and Pickett, 2009).

Strong arguments have been proposed that it is inequalities brought about within countries directly as a result of government decisions and policies that lead to the marginalisation and neglect of some groups in society. Such failure to prevent harmful inequalities arguably amounts to neglect of the state duty of care (Dorling, 2012; Lynch and Baker, 2005; Wilkinson and Pickett, 2009). Rather than working towards an equality of life condition for the maximum number of citizens, states pursue neo-liberal policies that lead to growing gaps between rich and poor, and by association between the autonomously literate and those with unmet literacy needs (Allen, 2007; Fahey, 2007; O'Toole, 2003). A radical egalitarian perspective suggests that only when all citizens are equally respected, resourced and empowered as learners, will these discrepancies diminish (Baker *et al.*, 2004; Lynch and Baker, 2005). In the course of this study on the role of care in learning literacy, this state duty of care emerged as a pivotal element in the learning care chain.

An ethnographic approach

Ethnography literally means writing about a people and is an approach to research with a commitment to accurately describing and explaining social contexts (Hammersley, 1995; Hammersley and Atkinson, 1994). In this case the people are a community of interest brought together by a shared experience of institutional abuse. Ethnography is a way of studying a group in depth and thereby accessing a new, hitherto hidden perspective on an aspect of social organisation. It involves becoming immersed in a community to the point where often-submerged meanings can be unearthed and shared as part of a natural relational exchange (Jeffrey and Walford, 2004). Feminists have highlighted the affective ingredient of the ethnographic process where it is neither possible nor desirable to remain aloof from community members (Edmondson, 2000).

Deep attitudes and ideas are expressed in the way people live their lives and memories are often expressed in the process of the familiar. This suggests that ethnography is important in the study of literacy that is understood as being socially situated, involving social practices and affecting communities as well as individuals (Alvermann, 2000; Florio-Ruane and McVee, 2000). Hodge (2003) describes how literacy ethnography allows the exploration of the particular in detail and involves:

> Studying a specific setting;
> Taking an holistic approach to whole phenomena;
> Employing a multi-method approach; and
> Maintaining contact with participants over a significant period of time.
> From an affective perspective, ethnography is therefore care-full in process and intent.

Memory was a core feature of this ethnographic process that focused on childhood recollection of literacy learning whilst in the care of the state. For groups that have been silenced and disbelieved, transformative change and healing can come from the act and process of narrating one's truth but the benefits of this process are not necessarily all one way. Writing about her narrative work with victims of the Northern Ireland conflict, Claire Hackett (2004; 2006) suggests that as well as the rights of memory and testimony there is also the right of audience; the right to be heard and to influence the future. Carspecken and Apple (1992), Carspecken (1996) and Cohen *et al.* (2000) explicitly describe *critical ethnography* as a process that moves beyond observation and description. Here the systemic roots of studied behaviour, of the truths gathered and shared, are articulated and the findings located within those systems so as to better promote emancipatory outcomes and structural change.

Literacy practitioner research

Practitioner research in adult literacy has been in existence since 1985 when the Research and Practice in Adult Literacy (RaPAL) group was formed. Based in Lancaster University, RaPAL was established to support inclusive practices in adult literacy work and promote learning democracy through ensuring that teaching, learning and research (and tutors, learners and researchers) are kept connected. Rooted in NLS[6] this approach to research aims to maintain a dynamic relationship between research and practice so that the meaning of literacy remains open and responsive to the variety of changing social contexts and practices that exist in our society. Practitioner research adopts a critical stance in relation to literacy policy design and particularly challenges decisions that are based on simplistic and mechanistic definitions of literacy (Hamilton and Barton, 2000; Fowler and Mace, 2005).

Ward and Edwards (2002) have highlighted the need to be conscious of the inherent power differentials in literacy practitioner research. In this regard Fowler and Mace (2005) also suggest that collaboration rather than intrusion can be achieved through openness and sharing the research question, process and outcomes with participants. They further advise incorporating elements of confidence building into the research so that the process itself becomes empowering. This is what Patti Lather named as 'research as praxis' and is characterised by negotiation, reciprocity and empowerment (Freire, 1972; Freire and Macedo, 1987; Lather, 1991).

Triangulation

Cohen *et al.* (2000: 112) cite triangulation as a powerful means of 'demonstrating concurrent validity' in qualitative studies. Originally a navigational technique that uses a number of markers to more accurately pinpoint a point on a journey, triangulation in data collection uses of a variety of methods and sources to check validity and reliability. This is particularly pertinent in ethnography where a single community of interest is being studied and the possibility of collective memory exists (Olick and Robbins, 1998). In this instance, collective memory referred to the socially accepted truth about life in industrial schools that was re-constructed through media documentary and repeated public narratives.

---

6. New Literacy Studies is discussed in some detail in chapter two

Such publicised accounts of the past, especially for those who forget as resistance, might bring into question the details of individual recollection. For this reason, a range of perspectives was important.

Challenges of the question

The nature of this particular enquiry required gathering data of an intimate and detailed nature not only about an individual's learning of literacy but also their experience of care. Each of these issues was sensitive and because of their stigmatised nature, much personal detail had remained undisclosed even to family members and close associates. In addition, reflecting on experiences of oppression, as part of a research process, can be painful and leave already damaged subjects vulnerable to further harm (Brewer, 2000). My overall intention was not just to avoid procedures that were destructive but rather to design a research process that produced robust data and was empowering and educational in its enactment and outcomes. The research design required a long lead-in. Relationships were developed slowly within which these searching conversations and disclosures might safely take place. Before engaging in the field, I also wanted to comprehensively validate the proposed question with literacy advocacy groups, tutors and learners.

Exploring the field

As suggested by Cohen *et al.* (2000) a considerable investment of time was needed to produce the most appropriate research design and site for this study. I initially spent twelve months facilitating learning with a range of individuals and groups with unmet literacy needs. During this time I reflected on the potential for research activity in each context. Prior work experience suggested a range of marginalised groups where literacy and affective inequalities might have been significant issues and so I began group and 1:1 work on a weekly basis with 1) young lesbian, gay, bisexual and transgender (LGBT) people, 2) women engaged in prostitution, 3) a disadvantaged inner-city community group, 4) homeless men and women, 5) survivors of institutional abuse and 5) an adult evening class for people who wanted to improve their spelling.

I was committed to an ethnographic approach and at the same time, while I selected a research site, the learning priorities of individuals and groups took precedence over a rush towards data collection. The literacy work, and the dialogue with tutors and learners, formed a basis for reflection, a kind of feasibility study that assured me there was a way to pose the question without causing harm to those who were vulnerable (Horsman and Norton, 1999). I had the chance to observe, gather information about and better understand the influence of previous literacy learning experiences in a range of contexts. There were many ways in which people's old learning patterns and behaviours re-emerged. These led to discussions about prior learning that were both empowering for individuals and informative for the research process. This real-time development of good learning relationships in turn impacted on levels of confidence and self-esteem (mine and theirs) and kept the preliminary research process grounded in the detail of the immediacy of learning. Where the horrors of the past revisited, sometimes they could be repelled by a new pattern and a new sense of possibility and so the research process was constantly alert to the potential for change.

I continued my discussions with learners and tutors about literacy, inequality and care. I ran some creative workshops with learners and again was reassured of the pertinence of the proposed topic of study. It was time to narrow the field.

Narrowing the field

It emerged organically and for a variety of reasons, that some groups were less appropriate research partners than others. In the case of homeless people whose immediate priority was shelter, participation in a research process over a stretch of time was unpredictable.

The weekly coming together of disparate individuals in an adult evening class solely and specifically for the purposes of improving spelling, was not conducive to the wider discussion and reflection that the research demanded. For these individuals who were taking time for literacy from already busy work and family schedules, participation in a lengthy research process was an unwarranted additional demand. Furthermore, within an inner-city community group, cultural boundaries around personal privacy were tightly drawn and respected and made this in-depth inquiry into sensitive issues overly invasive.

I felt that asking the women who worked in prostitution to reflect in greater depth on their care-less lives posed a high risk of being harmful and contributing to, rather than diminishing, their sense of worthlessness and exploitation (Edmondson, 2000). This was based on observations of the negative affect that participation in another research process had on some women. Revisiting past brutalities and neglects was disturbing and the aftermath long outlived the departure of the researchers from their lives. I rejected the idea of replicating this type of outcome.

Literacy was not an issue for the youth group although affective factors were immensely important and the group did participate in a subsequent affective study (Lynch *et al.*, 2009). There was anecdotal evidence that unmet literacy needs were significant amongst the older gay community where, in particular, feminised men had felt bullied out of the school system, but it was beyond the scope of this research to pursue that issue further.

After the initial exploratory period it became evident that the Lighthouse Centre for survivors of institutional abuse in industrial schools offered the best opportunity for further exploration of the research topic. Consequently, limitations of time meant that I was unable to continue working with all of the original groups and the issue of leaving the field emerged in relation to this preliminary process. Brewer (2000) argues that a researcher must always be cognisant of the rights and sensitivities of research participants and place these interests before the commitment to knowledge seeking. In this case, I maintained a literacy-tutoring role in some contexts where the collection of data would have been inappropriate but where disrupting the learning relationship would also have been untimely. In other contexts I ensured that contact with local literacy organisers was provided and alternative tutors put in place. This enabled me to increase my weekly time commitment with survivors from half a day per week to two days and thereby deepen relationships with literacy learners and other community members.

Why survivors of institutional abuse?

Survivors of institutional abuse, who met in their own community centre in Dublin, came from diverse backgrounds and yet were part of a solidary, supportive community of interest. High instances of unmet literacy needs existed amongst survivors for whom childhood had often lacked any form of stability or security. They came together to participate in state-funded, compensatory educational provision that acknowledged the harm caused to them through their earlier learning experiences.[7] Possibly for this reason, unmet literacy needs bore less stigma than in wider society and, like their early experiences of abuse, literacy biographies were constantly being openly discussed and processed within the community environment. Both of these factors made survivors of abuse in industrial schools appropriate partners in the collection of data for this project.

7. The admission of state responsibility for abuse and educational neglect in industrial schools is outlined in the statement given by the Department of Education and Skills to the Commission to Inquire into Child Abuse on 12 June 2006. www.childabusecommission.ie

During the year of preliminary literacy work in the Lighthouse Centre, I had already openly discussed my research with people and a number had volunteered to share their stories with me. The narratives that emerged naturally in the day-to-day life of the community had assured me of its suitability as a research context and I was happy that I had established a secure reciprocal relational basis on which to proceed.

The Lighthouse Centre was established in 1999 by a group of survivors to provide healing through adult learning opportunities; adult literacy was a core part of the work of the Centre.

Processing the past, rehearsing narratives and issues of memory

The Lighthouse Centre had a strong restorative culture of open discussion and analysis of past abuses alongside which the ethnographic memory work sat harmoniously. People were processing their recollections of past experiences in preparation for appearance before the State Redress Board, outlining their evidence to the Confidential Committee of Inquiry into Child Abuse and justifying application to the Education Fund because of past educational neglect. The majority of survivors were attending weekly counselling sessions and the processing of the past was sometimes rehearsed and repeated in the community setting. As such memory exploration was a natural part of the community environment.

The Redress Board was set up by the state as part of a number of measures designed to respond to allegations of abuse in industrial schools that began with a television documentary *Dear Daughter* in 1996. Under the Residential Institutions Redress Act (2002) the Board's role was to assess allegations of abuse in industrial and reformatory schools and other residential institutions named under the Act. The Redress Board would then make an offer of compensation to the applicant based on its judgment of the severity and degree of injury to the abused person. In exchange for the financial award, survivors had to agree in writing to waive any right of action against a public body or person and to discontinue any proceedings they may already have begun against them.

Three other measures existed to support survivors. Until the December 2005 deadline, they had an option to tell their story to the Confidential Committee of Inquiry into Child Abuse. It subsequently published a report on the evidence it had received that gave evidence of abuse described variously as systemic, pervasive, chronic, excessive, arbitrary, and endemic (Ryan, 2009). Survivors could also avail of the National Counselling Service and make application to the special Education Fund for their own or their family's compensatory educational needs. Each of these elements recognised a wrong done under past public administration and as well as implicitly acknowledging culpability, was also viewed as a form of remedial care for past neglects. Each service required an element of revisiting and processing the past.

My relationship with the Lighthouse Centre

The Lighthouse Centre was established to offer educational opportunities to residents of industrial schools and this was its core function. It did however have a broader social function as a community centre for those with a shared experience of institutional abuse. My inclusion and presence over the years in celebrations, outings and general day-to-day activities extended observations and discussions about literacy learning beyond the formal confines of the classroom or the research interview. My primary identity was that of unpaid literacy tutor and as such the offering up of narratives was generally construed and articulated by participants as a fair exchange and recognition for that role. As my research interest became known to centre users they volunteered to 'give their story' or helped to find those outside the centre who matched the age, gender and literacy status requirements of the sample. The process thus evolved into a reciprocal learning relationship where subject knowledge and analysis were exchanged for literacy tutoring.

Throughout the three-year ethnographic research process and beyond, my primary and enduring relationship with the group was as researcher and voluntary literacy tutor. This role was at times extended to include cover for the manager when he was on matrimonial leave or attending conferences. These occasions gave me an additional perspective on the services offered by the centre and affirmed and contributed to my position as a trusted insider. I chose to think of my position as maintaining *relationships of conscious distance* where affective bonds were naturally formed and the reality of my research and my role as literacy tutor both dictated the boundaries within which that contact took place and evolved.

Research design and methods

The ultimate study set out to explore the role of learning care in the realisation of literacy capability through the 'critical case sample' provided in the survivors of institutional abuse (Patton, 1990: 169). In particular the research sought to identify what type of care biography accompanied the successful acquisition of literacy or where literacy needs remained unmet, to clarify if this could be attributed to an absence of some particular aspects of care. In choosing to carry out the study with those who were resident in industrial schools it was hoped to reduce the number of variables presented by diverse family structures and status. Through examining the experience of those from a similar 'home' and learning environment it was hoped to isolate factors that supported or restricted the learning of literacy. This was possible to some extent but it was rendered more complex by the uneven patterns of care experienced by many whose childhood was in practice a chaotic blend of state care and family life—moving in and out of care on an erratic basis. On the other hand, this in itself produced interesting comparative data from individuals who had experience of institutional care and family life as well as learning in 'outside' (mainstream) school and 'inside' school within the institution.

Multiple research methods were deployed in data collection and these included participant observation and accompaniment in everyday contexts, sometimes through one-to-one literacy work. This literacy role was constant throughout the three-year research period and as well as being part of a reciprocal learning process it served as an interpretative base for subsequent in-depth interviews. I spent over 1200 hours in the field including literacy work, other *ad hoc* contributions to the centre, social activities and more direct data collection. I planned that my withdrawal from the field would take place as gradually as my entry began and this was the case. An extensive investment of time was necessary to avoid an exploitative or harmful approach to the work and to ensure access to the rich data that comes from genuine relations of confidence and trust built gradually and sustained over a considerable period of time.

In the course of day-to-day activities within the centre, my work progressively became a subject of interest and provoked the spontaneous telling of stories about learning regimes within industrial schools. Many of these were recorded as diary entries. After initial relationship building, in-depth individual interviews were carried out with twenty-eight group members (Table 1) some of whom are regular users of the centre and others who are recognised members of the wider community of interest but were in full-time study or employment. The interview process respected people's clear desire to have the opportunity to tell their story without the interruption or intrusion of others.

The data from interviews was complemented by a review of secondary documentary evidence including published reports and electronic transcripts from hearings of the Committee established to inquire into institutional abuse.

The personal narratives of survivors, both published and unpublished were also consulted (Doyle, 1988; Fahy, 1999; Flynn, 2003; 2003a; Ryan, 2009; Tyrrell, 2006). The data was further validated through methodological triangulation (Denzin, 1997) involving a further ten in-depth interviews with tutors, counsellors, legal representatives and others working closely with survivors of institutional abuse.

The research interview sample

Alongside other data collection, thirty-eight people took part in in-depth semi-structured interviews. Of these twenty-eight were survivors of institutional abuse and ten were professionals working in a range of capacities. All of the respondents were associated with the Lighthouse Centre and either attended regularly for educational courses or belonged to the wider community of survivors who are recognised as part of the community by its members. This member status is determined by having been for some period resident in an industrial school, a care home or in a few cases a medical establishment where abuse was known to have taken place.

Literacy profile

After the pilot study, all of those interviewed were within the forty-sixty-five age range and were equally divided between those whose literacy needs had been met at school and those who had finished school with unmet literacy needs. It was interesting to make some comparison between the care biographies of those who learned and those who did not learn literacy. Literacy is not a fixed entity and so respondents fell along a continuum of met and unmet needs. This was defined by their own subjective classification of their literacy status on leaving school. Some were clear that they had little or no literacy at this point and were in a number of cases unable to write even their own name. These I have described as 'unmet' needs. Others had some grasp of basic literacy but knew they had sizeable gaps in their knowledge and these I have called 'partial'. The remaining group felt autonomously literate and these are designated 'met'.

My presence over the years in the Lighthouse Centre allowed me to verify the literacy profiles of respondents. In only one case was it necessary to change a designation from 'met' to 'partial' and this was negotiated with the respondent.

Table 1: A learning care map of interviewees

Coded ID	Pseudonym	Age	M/F	Literacy status leaving school	Age going into care	Total years in care	Location	Educational qualifications[1]	Year gained
LF1	Laura*	59	F	Unmet	3	13	Cavan	Junior Cert	Current
MB2	Jennifer*	41	F	Unmet	7	18	St. Michaels	Junior Cert	1998
ML3	Susie	60	F	Unmet	3	13	Goldenbridge	Junior Cert	Current
JC4	Jane	57	F	Unmet	4	12	Goldenbridge	Primary Cert	1960
G/D5	Gill	46	F	Partial	In and out; fulltime at 4	13	Madonna House Goldenbridge Navan Road	IT Teaching Diploma	1997
OW6	Una	40	F	Met	Not disclosed	n/a	Dublin	Post Graduate	2006
C/D7	Carol	50	F	Met	In and out; fulltime at 7	10	Madonna House Booterstown Goldenbridge	Psychology certificate, NUI, Maynooth	2006
BF8	Bridget	51	F	Met	9	9	Goldenbridge	MSc	1996
CB9	Clare	59	F	Met	3 weeks	18	Baby Home Foster care Goldenbridge	Nursing and midwifery	1970
K/R10	Brenda	55	F	Met	5	10	Goldenbridge	Parenting Mentoring Diploma	2006

Table 1: A learning care map of interviewees (continued)

Coded ID	Pseudonym	Age	M/F	Literacy status leaving school	Age going into care	Total years in care	Location	Educational qualifications[1]	Year gained
T/G11	Pam	42	F	Partial	Birth	18	Drogheda Goldenbridge	None	
DA12	Dara	53	F	Unmet	6	2	Goldenbridge	None	
SM13	Sara	46	F	Met	5	3	Rathdrum Goldenbridge	Govt. training course	1990s
TC14	Tania	52	F	Met	2	14	Clare Limerick	None	
M/N15	Mona	51	F	Met	Birth	17	Tipperary Limerick Cashel	Leaving Cert	
GG16	Gary	53	M	Unmet	8	5	Goldenbridge	Leaving Cert	2006
DS17	Derek	52	M	Unmet	2	15	Passagewest Letterfrack Daingean	None	
DM18	Martin*	64	M	Met	Birth	16	Navan Road Stillorgan Carriglea Artane	Leaving Cert	1963
VC19	Vincent	54	M	Unmet	6	10	Tralee	Junior Cert	2004
BR20	Bob	41	M	Unmet	6	15	Booterstown	None	

Table 1: A learning care map of interviewees (continued)

Coded ID	Pseudonym	Age	M/F	Literacy status leaving school	Age going into care	Total years in care	Location	Educational qualifications[1]	Year gained
LC21	Liam	41	M	Unmet	3	1	Clifden Goldenbridge	Govt. training course	1990s
GM22	Gus	47	M	Unmet	3 months	17	Ballaghaderreen West Meath	Junior Cert	2004
PL23	Paul *	74	M	Unmet	6	12	Enniscorthy Artane	Junior Cert	2002
MC24	Matt	64	M	Met	5	9	Drogheda Artane	3rd level Access	2007
PH25	Jim	58	M	Met	9	7	Artane	Primary Cert	
GC26	Bill	48	M	Unmet	6	9	Galway	3rd Level Counselling	2006
PC27	Carl	44	M	Met	4	16	Goldenbridge	Group Cert City and Guilds Junior Cert	1978 1983
JK28	Kevin	56	M	Partial	7	9	Rathdrum Artane	None	
PS29	Counsellor		F	n/a					
AW30	Centre worker		M	n/a					

Table 1: A learning care map of interviewees (continued)

Coded ID	Pseudonym	Age	M/F	Literacy status leaving school	Age going into care	Total years in care	Location	Educational qualifications[1]	Year gained
SFG31	Legal		M F	n/a					
A/C32	Psychologist		F	n/a					
TK33	Tutor		F	n/a					
ED34	Centre worker		F	n/a					
SFG35	Tutor group		FFF	n/a					

* Denotes participants with whom the interview schedule was piloted.

1　Primary Cert and Group Cert no longer exist and were completed by those leaving school after primary education. Junior and Leaving Cert are still the main Irish school examinations corresponding approximately to GCSE and A Level.

Care biographies

The *learning care* map presented in Table 1 indicates the range of care biographies in relation to a number of factors. The variety of institutions attended provided representation across the industrial school system and included both rural and urban settings as well as the care culture of a number of different religious orders. Some participants had been in a number of different schools and made interesting observations about the variance in learning care that they experienced.

Respondents spent different lengths of time within the schools and this is recorded showing first age of entry and total number of years. By implication we can see the amount of time, if any, that respondents spent at home and how this relates to literacy status. Family contact was maintained with a number of children throughout their time in care and this had an important impact on their care experience. Although also unclear from the table, some in the sample had access to foster parents for weekend visits and holiday times and this made a significant care difference that impacted on literacy. A number of those interviewed were orphans and within the industrial school system they were reportedly the most stigmatised for their total lack of any of the benefits accrued from care.

Class, race, sexuality and capability

The sample was purposively selected in terms of gender and literacy status. In addition, a range of subgroups was randomly selected from within the pool of survivors. Two respondents were of mixed race. One man came from an Irish Traveller family. Two men identified as homosexual. Two women had mild learning difficulties and one man was dyslexic. The majority were Catholic but data was not gathered about current religious practice. With one exception, all of the respondents were working-class in origin.

Current educational status

Research participants' educational status, measured in qualifications, ranged from none to postgraduate level. A number were actively involved in basic courses to acquire equivalents of school-age examinations. Others had tried to pursue higher-level courses but although academically capable, were unable to take the emotional pressure of being in a group or sitting examinations. Many are content with informal learning and pursue a range of interests in this way.

The interviews

Given the sensitive nature of the interviews it was essential to put respondents at ease and to make clear their power within the situation. They were given control of the timing, pace and duration of the sessions. I was aware that survivors are often uncomfortable about rooms with closed doors and negotiated the location of the interview and the room layout accordingly. Respondents knew they could stop the process at any time and on a number of occasions I stopped the tape to allow emotional distress that arose in relation to their narrative, to subside. Respondents were always keen to continue and it was important not to silence, repress or stifle natural emotional responses.

At the same time, it was important to be mindful of the emotional costs of telling the story of significant past harms and to prepare for, support throughout and follow-up on the interview with each participant. In practice this meant dividing some interviews into a number of sessions, always ending on a positive note and watchfully accompanying the participant as they reintegrated into the community. I learned from the pilot study not to schedule interviews for the end of a day when participants would be going home alone to further reflect on negative experiences. Part of the process was to check for some time afterwards that there was no harmful fallout from the interview process.

I began interviewing more confident group members so that I was able to monitor the impact with them and refine the approach. This set up an informal peer support network and I frequently overheard participants discussing their conversations with me. Processing of the past was a natural part of the centre's culture and I did note an increased interest in literacy issues during the interview period. At this time it also became necessary to clarify why some group members were interviewed and others not, so as to avoid feelings of exclusion.

Respondents came back to me with additional information that they wanted to include in the data and a number said that the process had helped them to process their own thoughts about learning and care. One man who was working on his own written narrative of his life in care said he was able to recall a number of forgotten incidents and make new connections with the past as a result of our conversations. For those whose quest was to reconstruct lost identity, this type of retrieval was of great consequence.

Coding and analysis

All of the research interviews were transcribed verbatim indicating hesitations, laughter and other paralinguistic communication that affected the meaning of utterances. This was important where emotion was a significant factor in the subject matter of the research and something like an extended pause becomes more articulate than words. These non-verbal indicators have been left in cited data.

Transcribed interviews were coded and analysed using MAXqda one of the software packages for computer-assisted qualitative data analysis (CAQDA) that facilitate the organisation and analysis of ethnographic data (Dohan and Sanchez-Janowski, 1998). Once data are imported into MAX, it allows the creation of a coding tree that is dictated by the data rather than some pre-imposed theoretical framework. The transcribed data therefore led the shaping of the text. I was committed to an egalitarian perspective on literacy and care and so already held these code bases in mind but otherwise, data were allowed to dictate their own code branch and this process was completed before any process of reduction was undertaken.

MAX facilitates the mechanical aspect of coding but does not replace the cognitive activity that is the core of data analysis. Interpretation of utterances is supported by presence and participation during the original discussion. Emotional emphases and intent are remembered as a feature of the research relationship and this influences the way data are understood and coded. Where an instrument like MAX excels is in the processes of searching and retrieving data for comparison and in facilitating the writing of findings into the final research document.

Feedback and consultation about outcomes—focus groups

On completion of the data analysis, a final phase of dialogical data collection took place. This involved consulting with research participants in a series of focus groups that encouraged recall, reflexivity and at the same time built solidarity around the issue of literacy. Two groups were attended by fourteen respondents, eight men and four women. Others asked for feedback to be given outside of these times.

I made a short informal presentation to each group where I explained the emerging findings based on the initial coding. I presented these in the form of a series of mind maps representing 'learning care' as implied by survivors' narratives. The conceptualisation of equality as having economic, cultural, political and affective dimensions was part of the visual representation. I wanted to avoid revisiting the detail of abusive experiences and at the same time to confirm my assumptions. I also wanted to move our discussions into the transformative potential offered by the research. The focus around learning care formed the basis of lively discussion and participants voiced their interest in having 'other talks like that' in future.

In this way focus groups were used as a form of Freirean popular education: teaching and learning through dialogue and reflection that is directly linked to people's lived experience, in this case, of the learning care associated with literacy (Freire, 1972).

Affective considerations

As a piece of community-based critical ethnography, the study was grounded in critical theory and aimed to expose oppression and inequality. In so doing it was mindful of the core concern here with affective equality in the way that the research process was implemented. The study therefore built on established relationships of trust within the research base. The research into affective factors associated with literacy to took place in a 'homeplace' setting (hooks, 1990: 49) where participants felt safe in the company of peers and were in a context of relative power in relation to the researcher in terms of community status. The community location also ensured ongoing support of participants through existing community structures so that when difficult memories surfaced they were shared with sympathetic others.

Working within the Centre for a number of years allowed me some agency in the sphere of educational provision and the connections made between people and courses. I was able to pass on information about existing classes and support people to pursue new directions. Through one-to-one literacy I was well placed to support learners to move into drama, to write poetry, to read work in a large group and to make connections with others working on literacy in the Centre.

The research process visibly and transparently took place within the Centre and so encouraged discussion and raised awareness of literacy issues. Open conversations about past literacy learning allowed for more straightforward comparison of the interrelationship between those from comparable backgrounds who learned literacy and those who did not. The profile of literacy in the Centre was raised and the number of people asking for support grew. I was personally unable to respond to all the demands on my time and additional classes were put in place.

Costs, boundaries and gains

There were costs both to the researcher and the participants in investigating stigmatised and sensitive topics like care and unmet literacy needs (Cohen *et al.*, 2000). Both the subject matter and the ethnographic mode of inquiry were distinctly relational and so demanding in terms of time, effort, and energy. Caring research relationships involve attentiveness, presence, respect and responsibility that can be challenging and even stressful whilst at the same time allowing access to important data. Much of the detail of participants' narratives was deeply poignant and their courage and resistance all the more obvious in the process of its revelation. Some people became upset in retelling their learning and care histories while most also reported feeling empowered and even liberated by making new connections and reaching a greater understanding of their experience.

As Bubeck (1995) has indicated in the wider care context, these research relationships were both rewarding and burdensome for the researcher and involved hard work and emotional challenges. Professional support and supervision from a qualified counsellor helped me to maintain a vigilant distance in the emotional domain so as to better support the participants and observe the data. I had anticipated that this would be useful when the data collection and analysis intensified and availed of the service throughout the final year of the research.

Time was an overarching investment in this research and my position as a time-privileged 'retired' adult educator allowed me to make this expenditure through choice and in pursuance of my own intellectual goal.

Boundaries

Researching, interpreting and writing up this study involved developing an awareness of and taking responsibility for a number of important boundaries. As a woman who had lived most of her life in the north of Ireland the concept of territory, borders and safety were all familiar both in their geographical and metaphoric sense. The boundaries between researcher and researched, between writer and research subject and writer and reader were ever-present junctures at which the researcher might create rather than reflect reported truth. Both Brewer (2000) and Edmondson (2000) stress the value of reflexivity and reciprocity in the ethnographic process and I tried to facilitate and encourage this dialogue both with the self and others throughout the study.

This work was about the respectful negotiation of crossings at the safety barriers that people erected to protect them from harm. Alongside this was the maintenance of honest, learning relationships that were bound by professional and ethical codes of practice. Carrying out research with survivors of institutional abuse involved the careful removal of boundaries that silenced survivors about their experiences of care and learning literacy. This meant consciously redressing careless patterns of connection, believing and making important the narratives that people have shared, and doing so in a constructive and where possible, emancipatory manner.

Plus ça change—more of the same

The literacy narratives of survivors of institutional abuse in industrial schools formed a *critical case sample* within this project. This implies that in addition to its unique validity in the context of industrial schools in Ireland, the described experience also has resonance with that of other individuals and groups who currently have unmet literacy needs (Cohen *et al.*, 2000; Patton, 1980; 1990). The age cohort of survivors (forty to sixty-five years) who took part in the depth interviews corresponds to the dominant group with unmet literacy needs in wider Irish society (Department of Education and Skills, 2006). In other words, these findings are not just of historical relevance but rooted in the narratives and experience of current adult learners, their peers and their children. The findings supported the hypothesis that care is a primary factor in the literacy learning process and that where affection is absent, individuals and groups are unequally challenged to fully develop their unique blend of capabilities (Nussbaum, 2001). It also follows that because we are interconnected as human beings, we, civic society and the state, are all diminished by our 'collective failure' to achieve greater affective equality (An Taoiseach Bertie Ahern, 11 May 1999 as cited in Health Board Executive, 2002).

This was not just an historical or local matter. The Irish experience of education that was used to further disempower oppressed groups has produced echoes in other contexts, all of which offer insights into persistent contemporary basic educational inequalities. In Canada, New Zealand and Australia, there are similar accounts of aboriginal and marginalised people being taken into institutions where they were subjected to authoritarian regimes and extreme attempts to erase their cultural identity. A repressive regime of discipline and punishment like that described by Foucault (1975) was commonplace in many educational establishments in the first half of the twentieth century and was further intensified in institutions that were ironically part of the 'care' apparatus of a state. Parallel educational injustices are arguably still the lot of individuals and groups that are less cared for or cared about within contemporary social structures.

In this ethnographic study, learning care was explored through its absence from the lives of those for whom life and learning were the antithesis of affection. For these research participants, literacy outcomes mirrored the (often negative) levels of care in their lives. Although with less openly abusive expression, such disregard and harm continue in the care-less educational experiences that occur today and result in persistent unmet literacy needs in both developed and developing countries (UNESCO, 2006; Commission of the European Communities, 2008; OECD, 2009).

Chapter 2

Literacy and inequality

Fundamentally letters are shapes indicating voices. Hence they present things, which they bring to mind through the windows of the eyes. Frequently they speak voicelessly the utterances of the absent.
(John of Salisbury, 12th Century AD cited in Clanchy, 1979)

Introduction

Understandings of literacy have changed somewhat since John of Salisbury's twelfth century definition of a form of virtual connectivity. Nonetheless, in the early twenty first century, the relational miracle, enabled by encoding and decoding text and signs, remains intact. Today's definitions of literacy vary in scope and in the dimensions that they include in the concept of literacy. Some focus on limited mechanistic definitions of the traditional components of language, reading, writing and sometimes maths. Others prefer to speak of literacies, in the plural. These perspectives tend to be more inclusive and to include vernacular as well as élite uses of language and the contexts in which they are used. Similarly they recognise how new technologies have changed and expanded the concept of what it is to be literate in the multimodal, digital information age (Kress, 2010; Kress and Street, 2006; Lankshear, 1997; Lankshear and Knobel, 2003). The letters may now appear on an electronic screen or mobile phone accompanied by symbols, images and sounds but as in the time of John of Salisbury, they still connect us with the thoughts and ideas of others.

Early links between literacy and inequality

The tasks named reading and writing historically became a symbol of the elegance and refinement of the few that set the user apart from the uneducated masses. In England, by the twelfth century *litteratus* and *clericus* had already become confused and interchangeable terms describing those elevated above their antithetical categorical pairs—the illiterate laity (Clanchy, 1979; Tilly, 1999). Conversely, *illiteratus* and *laicus* were terms denoting those already stigmatised as ignorant and inferior for want of literacy skills. The learned, lettered and scholarly and those members of the church who were even minimally acquainted with Latin scripts, held status, prestige and usually power over the unschooled majority of the population. Throughout time these literacy-based divisions have remained deeply entrenched and although the identity of the dominant groups has altered, the associated inequality remains.

This chapter looks at conceptualisations and distributions of literacy across time and traces the connection, often unmarked, between literacy and inequality.

Throughout much of history, literacy has been viewed as an unquestionable and unambiguous good. This is not surprising as those defining that history belonged to a tiny minority who possessed these scarce, developed abilities. Literacy and progress became synonymous, and the objective of universal literacy was held up as the final milestone on the road to utopia (Graff, 1981). This understanding of literacy was (and still is) one that involves a mechanistic manipulation of language, and the ideas it carries, out of and into codes, in order to access and reproduce meaning. Across cultures, these codes are made up of letters or characters and in many languages they are interspersed with secondary symbols that indicate intonation and other aspects of meaning not carried in the writing system. The first recorded alphabet in 2000 BC has been attributed to the Arameans and the Phoenicians whose alphabet forms the basis of most written language today and whose trading also foreshadowed global capitalism. Early literacy was already bound up with the efficient recording of trading deals and the economic imperative of literacy remains important today (Sacks, 2003).

Writing about literacy in medieval Ireland, Jane Stevenson (1990) uncovers evidence of extensive varieties of written texts in Hiberno Latin and Hiberno English as well as the Irish Language. As early as the seventh and eight century Irish poets, *filid*, were recording their work and accounts of trading with the Roman Empire exist from the fifth century. Although in the medieval period literacy was usually concentrated around towns, in Ireland, it appears to have been more widespread and to have included vernacular uses of literacy that were uncommon elsewhere. As in other places, literacy was classed and gendered. Writing about early medieval Irish women shows that despite more favourable marriage laws where they had the right to dismiss an unsatisfactory spouse, they is no reliable evidence that they were more likely than their European counterparts to be literate or to involved in authorship (Peyroux, 1998; Stevenson, 1990).

The authority of the written word

By the thirteenth and fourteenth century, the mass of the population's only direct use of a book was for swearing on the veracity of their oral deposition to an ecclesiastical court. Memory of an event was not supported with written evidence but by presentation of a persuasive verbal account of recollections, for example of a legator's stated intentions. Records of such legacies show that medieval ownership and authorship of books was an élite and predominantly male preserve (Power, 1995). People gradually learned to respect the authority of the written word even when they could not read or write it themselves. The written word held knowledge, truth and with them, power. Books and the skills to decipher them remained rare and precious and were often the cause of suspicion as well as deference. Scarcity of printed materials made them, and the capital banked within them, the preserve of the rich and the religious. 'Rough' culture was without written record and by contrast something very local, passed on only by word of mouth (Leroy Ladurie, 1977; 1978).

History is humanity's capacity to document in writing its experience in the world and so the West has designated as 'prehistory' the age in which humans lacked the capacity to manipulate the written word. When the Spanish Conquistadors, in the fifteenth and sixteenth centuries, came upon peoples who preserved their traditions orally, not with the written word, they called them *'peoples without a history'*. This was tantamount to saying that most of the world's people are ahistoric and that it is literacy that allows a person, or people, to cross the watershed between oblivion and existence, between passing into obscurity and becoming a lasting memory (Instituto del Tercer Mundo, 2003). Literacy, thus, was attributed with the power of transcending time and individual ephemerality. The written word could outlive death itself.

The printed word

In the fifteenth century, printing brought new networks of communication, new choices for some people and new means of control for others. It also increased the power and division attached to literacy status. By the sixteenth century those who could read had access to greater numbers and variety of books. Literacy practices changed and the need for scholars to wander came to an end as copies of books existed in more widespread locations. Written texts began to be cross-referenced and this produced new permutations of old ideas and created new systems of thought (Eisenstein, 1968). The cleft between literate and illiterate widened. The production and reproduction of ideas and meaning continued to be the preserve of an élite few who named the world while the majority remained excluded and alienated from the process.

The impact of printing, and the associated commerce, gradually extended and reading skills became more widely sought after. Reading was taught first and separately to writing, reflecting the literacy demands of the time. It is assumed therefore that those who could sign their name were also able to read and literacy statistics from the eighteenth and nineteenth century were measured accordingly. There was limited shame attached to making you mark if you were unable to form letters and so there was no reason to feign literacy if you had not yet learned to crack the code. The ability to sign one's name established you as a literate person even if that skill was passive rather than active. The *passively* literate person could read but not write compared with the *actively* literate person who could do both. Making your mark as opposed to signing your name meant you were illiterate (Cressy, 1977; Mace, 1995, 2001; Spufford, 1979).

Jane Mace (2001), writing from a New Literacy Studies (NLS) perspective, has questioned the statistical accuracy of this method of measuring rates of literacy that omits relational factors. She provides evidence both from literature and historical documents[8] that suggests that neither marks nor signatures were reliable indicators of literacy status. Nervousness in the face of authority or an unwillingness to appear superior to another might cause a literate person to make their mark. Alternatively in France a signature might simply have been a sign that the *modèle* prepared for an individual by their writing teacher had bee carefully copied but could not be reproduced autonomously (Mace, 2001:46). Early statistics, therefore, are acknowledged to be merely indicative and somewhat unreliable.

Notwithstanding these flaws, this beginning of record gathering has allowed for some statistical estimates about levels of literacy and the changing social structure of literacy and illiteracy to be gathered retrospectively. The collation of information about those who signed witness testimonies in court, signed a copy of their will, signed applications for their marriage certificate, all gave indications about the spread and extent of literacy. Records gathered between the sixteenth and eighteenth century show that literacy was largely appropriate to social need, expectation and occupational requirement. Acquisition of reading and writing skills were strongly economically determined and heavily socially

8. In Charles Dickens's Bleak House (1852) a woman who can write chooses to make a mark in the marriage register so as not to embarrass her new husband who has less well developed literacy skills.

stratified and gendered with evidence that illiteracy was most common amongst labourers and women (Cressy, 1977). Increasingly literacy, over and above other intelligences became an essential lever of wealth, power and esteem. The first national report on literacy in England was published in 1840. It was based on statistics gathered from marriage registers and asserted that sixty-seven per cent of men and fifty-one per cent of women were literate according to the definition of the day. They had written themselves into the world by writing their name (Mace, 2001:49).[9]

Literacy and productivity

Prior to the introduction of compulsory schooling in the early twentieth century, concepts of literacy remained much as they had done since the sixteenth century. The normative expectation was that a person would be able to read a little and sign their name when required and the number of those in England who could satisfy these criteria passed the forty per cent mark by 1840 (Schofield, 1973). If limited literacy had become an effective means of ensuring social control and obedience to the established hierarchical social and religious order then industrialisation changed all this. Literacy became a requirement for a greater number of people as an essential ingredient in the growing economy. This shift led to the emergence of schooling for those in less privileged social positions whose labour and productivity became increasingly sought. The schooling remained patchy and was still often run according to the agendas of religious or charitable groups. It was usually fee-paying and for many people raised issues of opportunity costs when employment was available for younger family members. Nonetheless, as more people accessed elementary education, the number of those with basic literacy skills grew (ibid).

By 1918 compulsory elementary education had been introduced in Britain for children aged between five and fifteen. In Ireland, after the establishment of the new state in 1922, legislation was enacted in 1927 that made attendance at elementary school compulsory for those aged between six and fourteen. Free secondary education was only introduced in Ireland in 1967 and the school leaving age was raised to fifteen in 1972 and subsequently to sixteen by the Educational Welfare Act (2000). The rapid rise in UK and Irish literacy rates during the twentieth century was directly correlated to the free availability of schooling, the quality and appropriateness of that provision and an individual's

9. Mace cites evidence from the work of Vincent, David. 1993: *Literacy and Popular Culture: England* 1750-1914, Cambridge: CUP.

ability to take advantage of the opportunity to learn. These variables affected members of different social groups unequally. This means that today, as at previous points in history, literacy remains a resource that is more easily accessed and enjoyed by those with wealth, power, esteem and supportive learning relationships (Baker *et al.*, 2004; DES, 2005; Wilkinson and Pickett, 2009).

Literacy and measurement

The complexity of accurately measuring text literacy acquisition means that the data provided are often proxy estimates using years of school attendance or achievement of basic qualifications to assume literacy (Du Vivier, 1991; Instituto del Tercer Mundo, 2003; UNESCO, 2006). Measurements cost money and carry different meaning in rich and poor countries. Tests and outcomes are contested and often like is not compared with like (Hamilton and Barton, 2000). A restricted concept of functional rather than critical or situated literacy has continued to dominate national and international adult literacy surveys fostered by the OECD (OECD, 1995; 1996; 1998; 2000; 2010). These have claimed to measure literacy through performance of 'real life' tasks identified as essential in a given society, at a given period in time. Nevertheless all of these definitions are constructed without consultation with individuals and groups that experience unmet literacy needs. No mainstream definition of literacy could yet be said to form the basis for measuring the liberating capacities of literacy (Atkinson, 2012) or to be consensual (Hillyard *et al.*, 2003).

In addition to the tests based on a view of literacy construed as a cognitive ability and primarily focused on reading, International Adult Literacy Survey respondents were interviewed about their background and their uses of literacy at home and at work. Here literacy was considered as a self-assessable ability or set of abilities that includes reading, writing and maths. Findings from the self-assessment and the questionnaire-tested section of the study did not concur. Respondents' views of their own literacy levels were consistently higher than the outcomes measured in the tests. This raised issues about the reliability and validity of the measurement (Sticht, 1999; Hamilton and Barton, 2000). Given that the imperative was to discover the scale of unmet adult literacy need and design policy accordingly, the validity of the quantitative dimension of International Adult Literacy Survey was pivotal.

Sticht (1999) queried the allocation of research respondents to levels (1-5) based on an eighty per cent probability criterion. This meant that respondents had to demonstrate an eighty per cent probability of getting the average item at a given literacy level correct in order to be assigned to that level of skill. The essentially random choice of this measurement point also implicitly set the definition of 'mastery' of literacy at an arbitrary level. Setting the probability criterion at fifty per cent as other studies do, in the case of International Adult Literacy Survey would half the number of adults scoring at or below level one. The allocation of levels in this manner also ignored the capacity of many adults to score at a variety of levels on the range of tasks, for example where vocabulary or context was more familiar to their life experience. Both of these issues may in some way explain the discrepancy between scores and adults own perceptions of their skill level as higher and more satisfactory than the survey results showed. The OECD saw the discrepancy between the test and self-assessment measures as evidence that people are deluded about their own abilities rather than that the measurement instrument was flawed or designed to create a crisis of falling standards (OECD, 1995; Hamilton and Barton, 2000).

For all these reasons, I prefer not to dwell on the statistical aspects of literacy in/equality but rather to look at the potential for change offered by different ideological positions.

Contemporary literacy discourses and inequality

Mainstream literacy discourse since the OECD studies in the 1990s has been dominated by crises of falling standards and their economic implications for individuals and states. By comparison, the social, cultural and political consequences of unmet literacy needs have received only marginal attention and considerations of the affective dimensions of equality in relation to literacy remain embryonic. The alternative, predominantly deconstructionist approach of NLS is making an important contribution to challenging the mainstream message but does not, as yet, explicitly address the structural inequalities that continue to reproduce educational disadvantage. Altogether, neo-liberal, situated and even Freirean critical theories of adult literacy have made little impact on the reality of persistent basic educational inequalities. In practice, despite much government rhetoric, funding for adult literacy research and adult learning programmes remains relatively low and participation rates continue to be stubbornly unrepresentative of measured need. This stagnation may be rooted in a state of denial that it is layered structural inequality that perpetuates unmet literacy needs, rather than the repeatedly cited failure of individuals or educationalists to meet the literacy challenge.

So, what is the scope for social change and greater educational equality in the diverse conceptions of literacy?

Mainstream literacy discourse

By far the dominant literacy discourse for the past decade has been one of 'falling standards' and the perceived inability of the education system to furnish the market with sufficiently flexible and productive workers (Commission of the European Communities, 2001; Department of Education and Skills, 2000; OECD, 1992; 1995; 1997; 2000). The now well-thumbed IALS study of twenty countries (OECD, 1997) situated the USA, the UK and Ireland almost at the bottom of the functional literacy league tables. These measurements revealed in the region of twenty-five per cent of the US, UK and Irish population aged sixteen to twenty-five had not reached the level of prose literacy that would allow them to carry out the most basic reading tasks (OECD, 1997). Of the estimated 500000 adults in Ireland with unmet literacy needs, only eleven per cent have since engaged in any formal literacy learning (Department of Education and Skills, 2006; National Adult Literacy Agency, 2012).

In their analysis of the International Adult literacy Survey for Ireland, Denny *et al.* (1999) suggested that the relatively poor literacy performance was merely an age *cohort effect* where the scores of less schooled, older participants, lowered the overall mean. Subsequent studies do indeed show the overall Irish literacy trends in schools improving in relation to other EU countries but radically declining in schools in the most disadvantaged areas (Cosgrove *et al.*, 2003; DES, 2005; Educational Research Centre (ERC), 2004; Shiel *et al.*, 2001). So it becomes apparent that wider social patterns of inequality, and not just age, are reflected in the distribution of one of the most basic forms of educational currency. It is this currency that in turn unlocks the larger coffers of other forms of capital: economic, social and cultural, in its embodied, objectified and credentialised states (Bourdieu, 1986).

Mainstream measurements like OECD, PISA[10] and other such standardising approaches to literacy are contested both by critical literacy theorists and proponents of NLS. Although they are based on an unproblematised definition of literacy, such quantitative studies continue to determine the dominant discourses that inform educational and wider social policy and expenditure.

10. PISA—Programme for International Student Assessment, a three-yearly survey (2000, 2003, 2006, 2009, 2012) of fifteen-year-olds in the principal industrialised countries, tests how far students near the end of compulsory education have progressed in reading, maths and science.

Not only do these instrumental views fashion meaning about the nature and value of literacy, they also (without meaningful consultation) attempt to frame our understanding about the nature and value of those who are literate or not. Consequently the implication is allowed to persist that unmet literacy needs are caused by dysfunctional families and groups rather than by a failure in the state duty of care that should ensure basic educational equality for all (Hillyard et al., 2004).

Critical literacy

Prior to the 'invention' of the literacy crisis in the 1970s in the post-industrial US and the growth of a socio-cultural perspective in studies of language and the social sciences, *literacy* was a term reserved for historical and global reflections about economic and social development (Lankshear and Knobel, 2003). The work of Paulo Freire and his associates propelled literacy into the consciousness and vocabulary of western educators. His was a perspective that articulated the links between unmet literacy needs and oppression and highlighted the futility of endlessly obsessing with the mechanistic side of literacy (Freire and Macedo, 1987).

In contrast to detached, instrumental approaches to literacy, both feminist and Freirean educationalists cite the significance of the emotions and personal experience as a basis of critical reflection and truth-making about the direction of social change (hooks, 1994). Freire saw this *seeing* and *naming* the world as a vital precursor to meaningful, authentic literacy practice (Freire and Macedo, 1987). Words only took on relevance and authenticity as they were used to 'name the world' and describe the action for change, the *praxis* that was needed to make that unequal world more just. The *denunciation* of dehumanising, oppressing aspects of everyday reality was inextricably linked to the *annunciation* of the path to transformation and equally true for oppressor and oppressed both of which are dehumanised by their continued, unequal relationship (Freire, 1972).

Critical literacy is therefore about the *practice of freedom* and the antithesis of the *banking* form of literacy named and discredited by Freire (1972) but still alive and well in standardised/standardising educational practice and assessment. Critical learning requires a progression from ideology to pedagogy and then ultimately and importantly to agency. It is only by taking us to the point of action that words exercise their full power to evolve a more equal society in which literacy will cease to be so unequally distributed (Barr, 1999; hooks, 1994). Yet, despite much optimism around critical theory, the translation into practice proves problematic. Freire stressed that his pedagogical practice could not be automatically transposed onto other circumstances but needed to be part of a wider transformational context where conscious struggle for change is a present reality (Freire, 1972). For the most part now, adult literacy work in Europe and beyond takes place under the shadow of successive strategies that have increased productivity and competitiveness as their goals. Critical aspirations are consequentially restrained by funding imperatives and the demands of a core curriculum. Structural change is definitely not on the agenda.

In the parallel context of women's community-based education Joanna McMinn concluded that while feminist and critical pedagogies:

> ... provide valuable insights into pedagogical processes, neither seems to offer a strategy that can be grounded in a wider political context for remedying the inequalities of women's condition. (McMinn, 2000: 86)

It would appear that this claim also holds true in the field of critical conceptions of adult literacy.

In *Pedagogy of Hope*, Freire (1996) argued that neo-liberal discourses with all their talk of modernity are merely creating another ideology to be used by the dominant classes, which in turn cunningly silences counter-hegemonic challenges. Evidence on the ground suggests that valiant and often voluntary efforts in adult literacy have produced little more than a 'trickle-up' effect from literacy to higher levels of education or economic advantage. Unsurprisingly, for the most part, educationally disadvantaged adults remain unattracted to existing learning opportunities.

Recognising affective aspects of learning

Critical literacy theorists, like feminist educationalists did begin to articulate the need for relational aspects of learning to be recognised and valued. In her analysis of critical learning, hooks moves a step further than Aronowitz and Giroux (1993) to highlight the solidary and emotional aspects of learning. She insists on the need to revive the 'excitement' of the learning process—a collective, communal, affective event where the lesson is to learn to 'transgress', 'a movement against and beyond boundaries' so that education can really become a practice of freedom (hooks, 1994:12): hooks emphasis anticipates Freire's shift towards the solidary aspect of affectivity in his later work *Pedagogy of the Heart* where our interdependence in learning and living are given more central importance (Freire, 1997).

In *Pedagogy of the Oppressed* (1972) Freire had already stressed the need for teachers to 'love' what they do. He claimed that to be a good teacher one had to love others, to be attentive to their needs as unique persons and to provide them with the care to learn. This affective awareness is evident in much literacy work that bears Freire's influence although it tends to be overshadowed by concern with issues of power and cultural inequalities and to remain relatively unelaborated.

Both feminist and Freirean pedagogies respected and believed in the significance and reliability of the emotions in learning. Rooted in an understanding of our interdependence, feminist consciousness-raising groups and Brazilian 'culture groups' proceeded from the personal to the political, from conscientisation to praxis. The consciousness-raising group, like the culture circle identified reflection and dialogue as collective, relational processes in the struggle for democratic change. Weiler argued that in his earlier work Freire did not sufficiently problematise solidarity in that he did not address 'the overlapping and multiple forms of oppression revealed in reading the world of experience' (Weiler, 1991: 34). Where different levels of privilege existed within groups, Weiler argued that the process of naming these diverse forms and degrees of oppression might just as easily lead to discord as solidarity.

Critical literacy theorists' interest in the affective domain has focused largely on the role of care and solidarity between tutors and learner groups. As such, affective issues have been subsumed into concerns about culture and power and not been fully recognised as a central, discernible factor in literacy work.

New Literacy Studies

Since the early 1980's a critical, socio-cultural approach to literacy has led to an accumulating body of research and theory known as New Literacy Studies (NLS). This movement is part of a wider 'social turn' in literacy away from behaviourism and cognitivism (Gee, 1999). Using ethnographic research to explore and challenge the hegemony of the perceived, dominant literacy, NLS has worked to carefully build a picture of the diverse vernacular or 'local literacies' (Barton and Hamilton, 1998) that are deployed in people's lives. A core task of NLS continues to be bringing together ethnographic accounts of local community experiences 'that disturb the global homogenisation of literacy' (Clarke, 2002: 120). New Literacy theorists question the validity of studies like the International Adult Literacy Survey and the extent to which such studies provide really useful knowledge about literacy events in peoples' lives. Mary Hamilton illustrated one of the core concerns of NLS when she argued that we should be doing more to contest the solidifying international 'regimes of truth' that are fed by standardised assessment and testing procedures (Hamilton, 2000:7).

Drawing on an interdisciplinary approach, NLS have used different local and vernacular experiences of language and literacy to uncover the complexities that are obfuscated in the traditional, reductionist, and functional view of literacy adopted in OECD studies, econometric manipulations of OECD data and many mass literacy campaigns. This, in turn, upholds the Freirean precept that it is only in the familiarity and reality of individual life-worlds that the word becomes significant, authentic and potentially instrumental in bringing about change (Freire and Macedo, 1987).

NLS suggests that imposed, dominant definitions and assumptions about the meaning and usefulness of literacy may help explain many adults' reluctance to participate in learning (Street, 2001). The view of literacy as an autonomous gift to be given to people is questioned and a shift is proposed to an ideological understanding of literacy as a set of variable social practices that must be defined 'locally' and dialogically in the context of protagonists' lives (Hamilton, 2000). This involves a naming of diverse evolving worlds and the place of literacy within them. Indeed NLS looks at the wide-ranging formal and informal literacy practices that exist and proposes that there is not only one literacy but rather many literacies (Barton and Hamilton, 1998; Barton *et al.*, 2000; Giroux, 1987; Street, 2001).

Through socially contextualising and deconstructing literacy practices, NLS has sensitised us to the historical and power parameters in which literacy and the uses of literacy are defined. A studied concentration on what people do and are required to do during literacy events is useful and counterbalances the growing *literacy deficit* narrative. NLS has been criticised for an emphasis on the limiting 'local' to the neglect of the 'global' or 'distant' nature of some literacies (Brandt and Clinton, 2002: 2; Kim, 2003; Reder and Davila, 2005). Street rejects the need to dichotomise in this way and argues rather for an exploration of the hybrid literacy events and practices produced as the distant becomes (digitally) absorbed into the local context (Street, 2012). NLS continues to introduce a fresh, credible and critical perspective to literacy debates. In its challenge to the hegemony of functional, neo-liberal discourse it has provided a form of resistance and turned attention towards the social context in which literacy takes place. Greater recognition of the unequal nature of that social context may strengthen the important resistance element of NLS and create more fertile conditions for research and pedagogy as praxis (Lather, 1991; Lynch, 1999).

Unequal literacy outcomes are against the stated goals of each of the theoretical positions discussed above: neoliberal, critical and situated. At the same time, perhaps because the notion of equality generally remains vague and undefined, the correlation between the social gradient and educational achievements continues to be elusive and unrecognised. I suggest now that using the *equality framework* developed in Equality Studies, University College Dublin (Baker *et al.*, 2004; 2009) may provide the conceptual basis for more closely and usefully associating notions of literacy and equality.

Literacy from an equality perspective

We have seen that literacy has historically reflected wider inequalities in society. In the past the rich, the religious, the cultural and political élite and the merchant classes have all used literacy to assert their dominant position and to maintain the subjugated position of others (Clanchy, 1979; Graff, 1981; Mace, 2001). Today literacy also mirrors widening regional and global inequalities. Concern grows about boys' literacy (CCL, 2009; CEC, 2008). However it is disingenuous to present boys as an undifferentiated group when in fact it is working class boys in all ethnic groups and cultures who are likely to have literacy difficulties and leave school early. Middle class and upper class boys are not allowed to fail in school (Lynch and Feeley, 2009).

Inequalities are not simple or static as literacy tracks global in/equalities within and between nations. So within wealthy nations the disadvantaged are more likely to have unmet literacy needs and poorer countries fair worst globally in educational access and outcomes. Over one billion people are deprived of the right to any education and at the turn of the twenty-first century Latin America counted thirty million more illiterate people than twenty years previously (Chomsky, 2000). Across the globe, seven hundred and ninety six million adults have unmet literacy needs and seventy-four per cent of them are in southern Asia and Sub-Saharan Africa. Within these global disparities lie further gendered inequalities with evidence showing that women have a lower literacy rate than men in most societies (United Nations Development Programme, 2002, Table 22: UNESCO, 2006).

Closer to home, *illiteracy* generally defines part of the experience of the *other* poor, ethnic minorities, people of colour, Irish Travellers or those with learning difficulties and disabilities. For yet other groups literacy may be a less visible issue concealed behind more obvious causes and symptoms of oppression—survivors of institutional abuse, women who work in prostitution, many deaf people, young people bullied out of school because of institutionalised homophobia, people with addictions, prisoners, homeless men and women. These are inevitably:

> ... groups whose traditions and cultures are often the object of a massive assault and attempt by the dominant culture to delegitimate and disorganise the knowledge and traditions such groups use to define themselves and their view of the world. (Freire and Macedo 1987:13)

Unmet literacy needs are frequently a by-product of what Katherine Zappone calls this systemic 'weighty disrespect' for otherness (Zappone, 2003: 133) that persists throughout societies, impacts negatively on certain individuals and social groupings and is reflected in the culture and power structures of our schools. In a 1982 interview in Ireland, Paulo Freire said:

> We really don't have pedagogical problems, we have political problems with educational reflexes.   (Crane Bag, 1982)

Tackling these 'political problems' that result in literacy inequalities is the role of a wider emancipatory project. Although it remains a basic component of full democratic participation and self-realisation, literacy alone will not deliver equality.

Whether or not one accepts the accuracy of literacy measurement, the impact of unmet literacy needs on social and economic stability is proclaimed in national and international studies and is part of the rhetoric that underpins national policy on education, poverty, social exclusion and related issues (Department of Education and Skills, 2000; Morgan *et al.*, 1997; OECD, 1997; 2006; 2009). Much less clarity and unanimity exists in relation to causal and transformational aspects of unmet literacy needs. Nevertheless it should be clear that illiteracy is not something that occurs in isolation, without any recognisable pattern or root in the current organisation of social structures (Crowther *et al.*, 2001; Tett *et al.*, 2012). Research in prisons, with diverse minority groups and excluded men and women, points clearly to the need for a more holistic, contextualised approach to adult literacy work (Corridan, 2002; Morgan *et al.*, 1997; 2003; Owens, 2000; Ward, 2002).

Kathleen Lynch (1999) names and documents how liberal theories of equal opportunities merely reproduce and sustain inequalities in education systems. State managers, middle class parents' groups, teachers' unions and members have little or no interest in transforming the system that serves their vested interests. Lynch argues that only a radical and emancipatory approach to educational inequalities will be effective in bringing about just learning structures that end the disproportionate favour extended to those who are already privileged in society (Lynch, 1999: 287-309). In other words, as black women of colour also deduced, 'the master's tools will never dismantle the master's house' (Lorde, 1984:110-113).

Nor are limited literacy outcomes solely a matter of concern for those who are from marginalised groups. Research shows clearly that in unequal countries everyone is disadvantaged in terms of health, mortality rates and educational outcomes. As part of a far-reaching epidemiological and anthropological study, data from the PISA, the International Adult Literacy Survey and US Department of Education, National Center for Educational Statistics figures for fifty states of the USA were reviewed. The results showed incontrovertibly that more unequal countries and more unequal states had poorer literacy outcomes that those where there is greater equality. Income inequality was the determining and correlating factor for lower literacy scores independent of levels of poverty (Wilkinson and Pickett, 2009). They conclude that raising educational achievement is inextricably linked to reducing social inequality and that literacy is an equality issue.

An equality framework

A conceptual framework of equality (Baker, 1987; Lynch, 1999; Baker, Lynch, Cantillon and Walsh, 2004; 2009) describes five interrelated dimensions of in/equality. These identify the differences in life condition between individuals and social groups in relation to:

> resources,
> respect and recognition (allocating status),
> power,
> working and learning, and
> love, care and solidarity.

Each dimension has a role in the overall profile of in/equality and the patterning of the dimensions varies between individuals and groups according to their experience of disadvantage.

As well as these *dimensions* of in/equality, four key overarching social systems are named within which inequalities are structurally generated, sustained and reproduced. These broad *contexts* of in/equality are:

The economic system,

The cultural system,

The political system and

The affective system

They provide the macro, systemic environment within which the complex web of dimensional aspects of inequality are experienced by individuals and groups (Baker *et al.*, 2004; 2009: Chapters 2&4).

Equality is not static or inevitable, as suggested by some, but dynamically associated with personal and community history, life experience and agency in relation to the five *dimensions* (Baker *et al.*, 2004). More importantly, degrees of equality are intricately linked to, and determined by the extent to which societal structures across the four *contexts* are justly and fairly designed and administered in the lives of different individuals and groups. Viewed in relation to uneven literacy outcomes this framework suggests causal and consequential unequal allocations of wealth, status, power and care that need to be defined and addressed (Lynch and Baker, 2005).

An equality framework allows us to more accurately understand, describe and elaborate the potential of (radical) literacy work in Ireland and beyond. There is a highly interactive causal and consequential pattern to the way that inequalities impact on literacy. Those who experience resource inequalities in childhood are more likely to experience unmet literacy needs than are those whose material needs are comfortably met. They are consequentially also likely to suffer resource (and other) inequalities in adulthood. Those who belong to groups that are less valued in society are more likely than others to have unmet literacy needs and to be consequentially culturally (and economically) disadvantaged in later life. So also other structural inequalities of power and care will contribute to educational disadvantage and cast their shadow forward causing political and affective inequalities in adulthood. Many groups and individuals with unmet literacy needs experience all of these aspects of inequality concurrently layered by generations of injustice in their families and communities.

The interrelated nature of the dimensions and contexts of inequality suggests that only a cohesive structural approach will bring about the type of root and branch change that will impact on persistent educational disadvantage. Because much of what is described as critical literacy practice fails to make the connection to any critical agency, its emancipatory potential remains untapped. Perhaps consequentially, adults are unmotivated to engage or persist in learning that perpetuates and heightens their oppression and so adult literacy programmes remain limited in their appeal, their reach and their impact.

Defining literacy in an egalitarian context

Freire and others have argued that to be meaningful, adult literacy needs to be contextualised in a wider debate and struggle against injustice. In the current context of floundering capitalism, economic depression and austerity, a move towards equality and social justice is not evident in the political thinking of many states. In national strategies, literacy is reduced to a miserly concept limited in scope and content to what is 'safe' for the preservation and reproduction of an unequal social order (Street, 2012: 27). Mostly we are left to imagine what literacy would look like as part of an agenda for a more egalitarian education system within a more just social structure.

Building on the multidimensional conceptualisation of equality discussed above, a definition of socially situated literacy might go something like this:

> ... the full range of text and language capabilities that facilitate the acquisition and use of all forms of economic and cultural capital and enable full and fair management of relationships of power and intimacy.

Defined in terms of in/equality it becomes clear how and why unmet literacy needs relegate individuals, families and entire groups to the margins of society. Educational disadvantage limits employment prospects and in turn threatens economic security. As well as being part of the culture of any society, language and literacy is the vehicle through which much cultural activity is carried on. Unmet literacy needs stifle creativity and important aspects of self and group actualisation. Critique and dissent are muffled if not altogether silenced. Those who cannot use literacy are less likely to vote, to take part in community organisations or to influence decision-making processes that affect their lives. At the same time their access to equality of condition with others across all institutions and structures is seriously limited and public and private relationships may be subject to stress and frustration.

Above all, as we explore in the next chapter, literacy is relational. The mnemonic function of literacy facilitates the relationship between the self and the world outside the self. Through reading we access the ideas and messages of others whether casually in scribbled notes from loved ones and peers or formally through the printed and published word. We encode messages as a means of creating, recording, exchanging and managing ideas and information with individuals and institutions from the most immediate to the global. Literacy is the vehicle for language that connects across continents and centuries, classes and cultures. We use literacy to move outside our own heads. We use it to connect and communicate, to dictate or to dialogue. We use it to sustain, participate in and critically develop organisational structures and to uphold and nourish our interdependence. We use it for obedience and compliance as well as for critique, struggle and resistance. If we cannot use literacy we, and our dependants, are affectively disadvantaged and consequently at greater risk of marginalisation and oppression than are literate peers.

Conclusions

By linking literacy and equality we are not just highlighting and struggling to end an unequal distribution of skills and capital building capacity to disadvantaged individuals and groups. This potentially deficit approach forms the basis of most adult education policy and implies that redressing unequal literacy distribution will in turn sort out other dimensions of inequality. Literacy alone, like education in general, is not emancipatory. Such a view fails to look at the wider implications of the relationship between literacy and the complex, interconnected patterns of in/equality of resources, power, culture and care.

Neglecting the wider context in which literacy happens, unwittingly contributes to the maintenance of inequalities that are rooted in social structures rather than in stigmatised individuals and groups. A radical egalitarian view of literacy could provide the theoretical base upon which to build more meaningful and relevant literacy practice. It would obviously have far-reaching implications for the way in which literacy work takes place but first and foremost, it may mean that the many adults who have been denied the right to use literacy would see some point in participating in lifelong learning.

Gardner (1999) questions why we prioritise literacy acquisition and measurement over achievement in the domain of other intelligences. We do not attach similar significance to national statistics for those who have or have not developed their musical or spatial intelligence or to those who have or have not achieved proficiency in interpersonal and intra-personal intelligence. These latter two may be argued to be at least as crucial to personal, community and national development as literacy skills and yet they have not been elevated to the same élite heights as have command of mechanical literacy skills. Perhaps literacy's early association with economic development has overshadowed the less recognised and undervalued function in maintaining relationships of love, care and solidarity. The next chapter turns in that direction.

Chapter 3

Why affective inequality matters

Caring is better understood… as helping individuals to meet their basic needs and to develop and sustain those basic or innate capabilities necessary for survival and basic functioning in society, including the ability to sense, feel, move about, speak, reason, imagine, affiliate with others, and in most societies today, read, write, and perform basic math.

(Daniel Engster, 2005)

This chapter looks at how care interconnects with other aspects of equality in the learning of literacy. The general neglect of the affective domain is strongly echoed in traditional analyses of unmet adult literacy needs where economic causes and consequences dominate most debates (Moser, 1999; Parsons and Bynner, 2002). Beyond the purely economic focus, cultural, social and political aspects of literacy have been highlighted through Freirean critical literacy theory and the increasing body of work done in NLS (Barton, 1994; 2007; Barton and Hamilton, 1998; Crowther *et al.*, 2001; Gee, 1999; Hamilton and Hillier, 2006; Hodge, 2003; Lankshear, 1997; Lankshear and Knobel, 2003; Street, 1999; 2012; Tett *et al.*, 2012; Tusting, 2003). This widening of literacy perspectives is important and welcome; nevertheless, it by no means provides the complete picture. The vital role of affective matters in literacy learning and use remains relatively unrecognised even though literacy events do much to facilitate us in being part of one another—endlessly and irrevocably interconnected (Engster, 2005; 2007).

The affective domain

Baker *et al.*, (2004: 61) describe the role of the affective domain as providing and sustaining relationships of love, care and solidarity. This takes place through systems and institutions like the family, community, friendship networks and care-giving institutions like children's homes and care homes for older people. The affective domain includes relationships of love and care where the love labour element can be both pleasurable and grindingly laborious. It also includes the relationships of solidarity that bond people collectively and voluntarily in variable degrees of common cause from simple recreational motives, to mutuality of community interest or the wider struggles against global oppression. All these aspects of care can be present (or absent) in a single relationship.

Lynch *et al.'s* model of *Concentric Circles of Care* (Figure 3.1) helps illustrate the sphere of influence of affective relations whether private or public, or as a paid or unpaid activity (Lynch *et al.*, 2007). By naming the different types and intensities of affection they offer a language for systematically interpreting the empirical data and more precisely describing diverse types of caring relationships. Elsewhere, Lynch and Lodge (2002:11) argue for schools and other places of learning to be recognised as 'affective enterprises' where both teaching and learning are deeply and variously concerned with relationships of care and interdependence. The boundaries of affective influence on learning literacy extend far beyond the school itself and are strongly connected to wider relationships and duties of care in the home, community and other social structures. This more precise understanding of the locus of care provides a useful base from which to begin to frame an understanding of the relational dimensions of literacy *learning care* in general and in the specific context of industrial and reformatory schools.

Figure 3.1: Concentric Circles of Care (Lynch *et al.*, 2007)

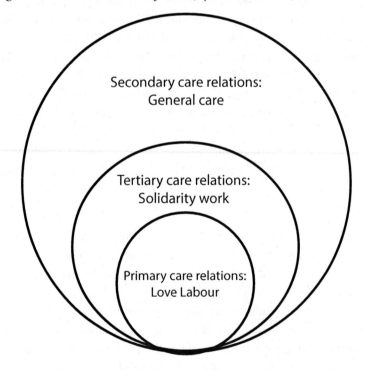

Secondary care relations:
General care

Tertiary care relations:
Solidarity work

Primary care relations:
Love Labour

Learning care

In this chapter the focus will be on evidence about elements of what I term *learning care*.[11] The term has been coined here to denote the attitudes and the actions, both paid and unpaid, that dynamically influence individuals and groups in learning literacy. Drawing initially on the work of Lynch and McLaughlin (1995), literacy learning care may be seen as part of primary love relationships between parents and children or between adults with literacy needs and their loved ones. This is where support for learning is part of a more general (unpaid) interest in the well-being of a loved one and an integral aspect of 'love labour'. Noddings (2007) argues that we all know intuitively about the pivotal importance of such care in learning but that it becomes obscured by other agendas and is rarely considered an issue in educational philosophy.

Learning care may also be a commodified facet of a relationship of care work in a childcare, pre-school or formal education setting (Lynch and McLaughlin, 1995: 250). In adulthood also, learning care may be located in a loving relationship that transcends the barriers created by poor schooling. It may be the positive caring approach experienced as part of an adult literacy scheme or personal development programme or a solidary community or workplace learning group. As well as involving effort, learning care is also about intent and attitude. It describes a desire for an individual or group to develop their literacy capability that is conveyed in attentiveness, responsiveness and respect in all aspects of the learning care work (Engster, 2005).

It is suggested here that the emotional poverty that results from care inequalities has a major adverse influence on the learning of literacy and all the relationships that literacy should subsequently facilitate. Inevitably, these literacy-linked affective inequalities are intricately causally and consequentially related to the more recognised inequalities of resources, power and status. Indeed proficiency in literacy may be said to underpin and influence the flow of all forms of capital—economic, cultural: in its objectified, embodied and credentialised forms and social capital that is the product of successful relational activity (Bourdieu, 1986). For this reason, in the three sections that follow, I will build a model of the 'dynamic cycle of learning care' that focuses not only on inequalities of care related to literacy but also on how these affective inequalities

11. The concept of learning care and learning care labour is based on the ideas of Lynch and McLaughlin (1995) in 'Caring Labour and Love Labour' where they distinguish between types of emotional work and the extent to which both may be motivated by solidary intent.

interface with other dimensions of inequality in terms of resources, respect and recognition and power. Inequalities in literacy learning are presented as a care problem that is intrinsically linked to inequalities of resources, power and status. From a NLS standpoint this involves a 'care turn' towards the affective aspects of social practice.

Care is an emerging link

There is an increasing body of interdisciplinary attention given to aspects of the affective domain in education. Recognition that facilitating learning is affective as well as cognitive is growing as focus falls on the attentiveness, commitment, compassion and other relational facets of skilful learning support.

In the USA and Ireland empirical and theoretical studies have examined the need for an ethic of care and for issues of affectivity to be an integral part of the school curriculum (Cohen, 2006; McClave, 2005; Noddings, 1992; 2006; 2007). In particular, these studies suggest that care is too important to be treated as an implicit aspect of other curricular areas but rather needs to be carefully theorised and articulated with learners and teachers. Hargreaves highlights the extent of teachers' emotional labour in research carried out with fifty-three elementary and secondary teachers in fifteen diverse schools in Ontario. He describes emotional geographies—forms of distance and proximity that can impact on the emotional understanding between teachers, students, parents and others in the learning process (Hargreaves, 2000; 2001).

Others approach care from an equality perspective arguing that structural inequalities of care are a pivotal and neglected area of the educational landscape (Lynch and Baker, 2005; Lynch *et al.*, 2007). Egalitarians link the feminised nature of care to its misrecognition within education systems dominated by notions of rationality, neo-liberalism and accountability. The unequal division of educational care labour is also illustrated in studies of mothers' work to support school-age children and the impact of a range of capitals on the resources they can bring to this task (O'Brien, 2005; 2007; Reay 2000).

The common thread in these various perspectives is the unrecognised, but vital presence of affective relationships in sustaining all human endeavours, including the lifelong processes of learning, formal and informal. A study of care in the field of adult literacy adds to this body of writing and considers the nature of the educational experience and outcomes when care is absent.

Literacy, care and resources

A *dynamic cycle* links resources, learning care and literacy. As well as being emotional, to be useful caring in the context of learning literacy also involves agency. Learning care work requires human resources of time, health and knowledge. It may also involve material and environmental resources of place, toys, books and increasingly, technological learning aids. Economic issues ultimately influence the degree to which all such learning care resources can be deployed to support educational care work.

Figure 3.2: *Resources* in the dynamic cycle of learning care

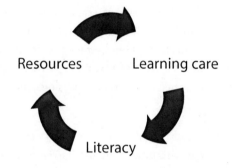

As repeated analysis of international literacy survey performance shows, unequal access to income, that in turn enables *learning care labour*, has a knock-on effect on the capacity of individuals and groups to reap the benefits of learning (OECD, 2006; OECD, 2011). Inequalities in life circumstances mean that those who access only impoverished learning care, whether in the public or private sphere, cannot match the learning outcomes of those to whom quality affective support is readily available (Lynch and Baker, 2005). As accounts of learning while in institutional care suggest, at the negative end of the care continuum, those for whom learning care labour is altogether lacking are unequally challenged to achieve and retain even basic levels of literacy (Raftery and O'Sullivan, 1999). This systemic educational inequality in turn impacts on subsequent employment prospects and earning potential, determining future patterns of care and learning and generational cycles of privilege and affluence (Harmon and Walker, 2003).

Literacy as a resource

In the previous chapter the scant recognition of equality in general in literacy theory and in particular the affective domain, was discussed. A number of egalitarian theorists have shown the links between literacy and general inequality mainly as an unequally distributed resource. Martha Nussbaum (2000) specifically raises the question of gender inequalities in the distribution of literacy, in the development context. However, for the most part this focus has been prompted by quantitative data that illustrates the extent of broader educational inequalities. Literacy itself has not been the central concern for her or others coming from an equality perspective (Baker *et al.*, 2004; Chomsky, 2001; Lynch, 1999; Nussbaum, 2000; 2001). Nussbaum's theory of central human capabilities, echoed by Engster (2005) cites literacy as a minimum expectation of compassion in public life (Nussbaum, 2001: 401-454). In taking this perspective she raises the issue of the state's affective role in literacy provision that will be explored further on in this chapter. Otherwise, up to this point, the affective domain and learning literacy have not been more than a passing concern for egalitarians.

Literacy, earnings and care

In the learning of literacy, until now, care has been an *unobservable*[12] and immeasurable factor in the dominant mainstream learning/earning cycle. Literacy and earnings, on the other hand, are intensively studied by those whose dominant concern is the economy, economic returns to education through employment and the implementation of the Lisbon Strategy and the subsequent *Strategic Framework for European Cooperation in Education and Training: ET 2020* (Commission of the European Communities, 2000; 2010; Denny, 2002; Harmon and Walker, 2003). EU agendas have been largely output-focused and as the league table culture gradually invades the education system with the pressures of performativity, any time and impetus to care for diverse learning needs is being eroded (Ball, 2003). Concerns about productivity and capital are squeezing out any investment in the caring aspects of education. In such an economically dominated climate, learning care labour is increasingly becoming a private matter and inevitably those who cannot supplement the system from their own resources suffer the greatest disadvantage (Baker *et al.*, 2004; Lynch and Moran, 2006).

---

12. The term unobservable is used in economics to denote concepts that are not measurable and may consequently be ignored.

From another perspective, this link between general education levels and earnings is also well documented by egalitarians whose priority is the move towards people-centred, just societal structures rather than productivity. Educational inequalities and their economic and social consequences for individuals and groups are well researched by many who acknowledge the economic and cultural power vested in education (Baker *et al.*, 2004; Healy and Reynolds, 1999; Lynch, 1999). Kathleen Lynch (1999) instigated debate about the nature of care in education and the struggle between capital and care for individuals and groups in the domain of learning. She makes the point that the concept and practice of care is highly gendered and because that which is feminine is of lesser social value, affective matters have not been taken seriously as a facet of learning.

> It is undoubtedly the case that caring has been hidden behind capital, and the resources, skills and capacities needed to care have not been seriously examined.   (Lynch, 1999: 278)

More recently an argument for the need to invest in the care environment of young children has emerged from the hiding place 'behind capital', and precisely to promote the interests of capital. Economists Heckman and Masterov (2004) have fashioned *The Productivity Argument for Investing in Young Children*. In this parental deficit thesis, they argue that schools cannot remedy...

> ... the important role played by disadvantaged families in producing less educated and less motivated persons and in producing persons more prone to participate in crime.   (Heckman and Masterov, 2004:34)

Without identifying systemic resource inequalities as the root cause, disadvantaged parents are held culpable for literacy gaps opening up long before formal schooling begins. Heckman and Masterov do not argue for greater economic equality so that parents can afford to devote more time to their children's development. Affective considerations are entirely excluded from the *Productivity Argument* and its ultimate objective. They argue that investment in preschool programmes gives higher returns than later educational interventions and that the economic efficiency argument for early childhood investment is more powerful and compelling than the traditional grounds of fairness and equity (Heckman and Masterov, 2004).

Like Lynch and Baker (2005), Noddings (2007) also acknowledges the inability of schooling alone to make an impact on persistent structural resource inequalities. She suggests that schools should at least try to provide equal and 'adequate facilities for all children [and] long-term caring relationships that support intellectual development' but doubts that there is enough will in society to allow these material and affective resources to be fairly deployed (Noddings, 2007:196-197).

The mainstream econometric focus on literacy has failed to fully consider the impact of an affective variable. At the same time, the growing egalitarian focus on education that has justly argued to give learning care labour its place along side resource imperatives has not as yet turned its focus specifically to the field of adult literacy.

The costs of learning care labour

Chapter two has shown that literacy, as a most basic educational outcome, has historically been a measure of individual wealth and status and a global indicator of a country's current and potential level of economic development (Anderson, 1965; Instituto del Tercer Mundo, 2003). In Ireland as elsewhere, illiteracy, poverty and unemployment are strongly correlated (Educational Research Centre, 2004; Kellaghan *et al.*, 1995; National Anti Poverty Strategy (NAPS), 1997; 2002; Parsons and Bynner, 2002) as resource inequalities impact causally and consequentially on every aspect and level of learning and employment opportunities. The role of learning care in this cycle is not articulated.

Against the backdrop of unevenly distributed economic growth, those who are poor are held back in a competitive education system that favours those who can deploy financial (money), material (things), human (people), corporal (health and well-being) and temporal (time) resources to sustain their learning advantage (Deegan *et al.*, 2004; Lynch and Moran, 2006; O'Brien, 2005; Wilkinson, 2005, Wilkinson and Pickett, 2009).

Health and literacy have been shown to be interrelated (Feinstein *et al.*, 2003; Wilkinson, 2005). Health and general well-being are also fundamental resources for full participation in lifelong learning and adult literacy has emerged as a significant determinant of child health, development and educational outcomes (Dasgupta, 1995; OECD, 1997; Wise and Signal, 2000). It is argued that adults with unmet literacy needs are more likely to have unresolved physical and mental health issues although the claim has been questioned by those who dispute the validity of standardised literacy measurement (Hamilton and Barton, 2000). The relationship between adult literacy and health has not been undertaken from a critical standpoint although a study of the benefits of lifelong learning generally does suggest that it can make a positive impact on the lives of individuals their families and community (Aldridge and Lavender, 2000).

The resource benefit that financial security gives to young learners means plentiful supplies of educational toys, books and technological learning aids in the home. In addition to these material resources, economic privilege increases the human and temporal investment parents are free to make in their children's future. Noddings (2007:191) argues that because some parents are unable to be educational role models, in the interest of justice and equality, teachers must undertake this role.

> Because so many parents, despite their love, cannot provide models of what it means to be educated, teachers must serve this function in the lives of those children. They must represent whole persons, not just instructors, in their relations with students. Students need to see the possibilities advertised as inherent in education are real possibilities for their own futures.   (Noddings, 2007:191)

This raises unresolved issues about the inalienability of (learning) care and how that work can be fairly distributed (Fineman, 2004). In privileged circumstances, mothers' and fathers' costly and time-consuming emotional labour inculcates children into the education culture and supports them to learn and to value the importance of credentialised capital (Allat, 1993; Heath, 1983; Noddings, 2007; O'Brien, 2005). Conversely, those who are economically disadvantaged possess less human, material, temporal and corporal resources and correspondingly less accrued cultural capital to invest in young learners. Children from more privileged backgrounds learn to read, write, use language, and understand the world and how to take their place in it. Economically, culturally, politically and affectively, they are provided with choices because their families have already an established stake in these structures and can work them to their advantage (Allat, 1993; Standing, 1999).

International research and local studies affirm that as a result of learning support in the home, many children can already read, or are well disposed to learning by the time they reach primary school (Department of Education and Skills, 2005; Heath, 1983; Educational Research Centre, 2004; Eivers *et al.*, 2005). Literacy inequalities are therefore already established in the first days of primary school (Lee and Burkham, 2002) and accelerate as perceptions of 'fast' and 'slow' readers emerge and begin to influence determinations of ability and learners' self esteem. The main determinant of these early educational inequalities lies in inequalities of economic and cultural capitals that in turn restrict the capacities to provide early learning care. Solutions to this are increasingly framed by 'family literacy', or more often 'good mothering' discourses that focus on increasing family pedagogical resources rather than the underlying, decisive resource issues.

> The practice of targeting family literacy policies towards those who are often most marginalised from the school system is another way in which families with the least resources and representation in the school system are encouraged to 'take responsibility' for their situation.
>
> (Smythe and Isserlis, 2003: 15)

Redressing generational literacy inequalities is essentially a matter of national expenditure targeted at redressing socio-economic inequalities. Those who have access to quality pre-school provision benefit from the essential linguistic enrichment that a child needs in order to learn the symbolic and decontextualised use of language preparatory to literate behaviour. For the most part, at both primary and secondary level, current evidence suggests that those who are least economically and educationally advantaged are carelessly concentrated into under-resourced learning environments and schools that minimise rather than enable and expand their future prospects (Brighouse, 2003; Fecho, 2001; Lee and Burkham, 2002; Lynch, 1999; Van Galen, 2004).

Pressures on families are not just centred on literacy itself but on mediating the relationships that maintain and support the entire schooling process. Management of the relationship between child and school requires time and know-how that is intricately linked with and determined by having adequate resources. Parental privilege and time allows mediation between the school and the child in a manner that the low-paid, double-jobbing, educationally disadvantaged and often solitary parent finds more problematic (O'Brien, 2005; Reay, 1998; 2000; Standing, 1999). Resources therefore layer advantage upon advantage for those from better off backgrounds and are pivotal in underpinning many of the factors that determine success in literacy learning and use. The resource-activated *dynamic cycle of learning care* (Figure 3.2) is reproduced in families and groups where the operation of capitals is familiar and learning care labour can be given high priority. Long before they enter formal schooling, the inequalities of condition, that mean some children will fail to realise their literacy potential, have already made an indelible impression. The literacy gap is firmly established.

Generational aspects of literacy, care and resources

Having put down roots in early childhood, in adulthood the cycle of disadvantage becomes evermore complex. The causal and consequential chain of links between poverty, learning care and literacy become clear in studies of family life on a low income. Where parents have unmet literacy needs, involvement in their children's learning, in both the public and private spheres, becomes an additional emotional pressure on top of already burdensome lives (Daly and Leonard, 2002; O'Neill, 1992; 2000; Smythe and Isserlis, 2003). Parents who described themselves as 'hardly [able to] read and write' reported conflicting emotions about their children's education (Daly and Leonard, 2002: 86). They recognised learning as a way of breaking out of the vicious cycle of disadvantage and wished for their children to do well at school in order to improve their future life chances. At the same time they felt powerless about supporting and assisting in many aspects of that process.

The researched, but unrecognised, widespread nature of unmet adult literacy needs in many communities is matched by a stubborn lack of understanding about the ensuing difficult reality of children's unequal lives as learners. When a study from the Irish Educational Research Centre (2004) reported that over thirty per cent of children in Ireland who attend schools that are designated 'disadvantaged', have serious unmet literacy needs, this was seen as a pedagogical rather than an economic issue. The immediate official response was to suggest more frequent testing in schools. This follows a wider neo-liberal trend in literacy that, rather than tackling causal resource inequalities, sees stringent, prescriptive national curricula and literacy tests, league tables and more targets for teachers as the cure-all (English *et al.*, 2002; Hamilton, 2000). In this way resource, educational and other interlinked inequalities are sustained and reproduced in lifelong learning practices and literacy care labour goes unrecognised and unresourced.

The evidence suggests that care plays an important intermediary role between inequalities of resources and literacy outcomes. People with fewer resources are squeezed in the learning care they can give, or command for their children. This in turn limits the preparedness of these children when entering school and the support they get from their families while at school. It means that some children require additional affective support that teachers find hard to resource amidst other legion demands and pressures. In adulthood, people with fewer resources can be constrained in the investment they are able to make in developing their own literacy needs and in the emotional support available for them to do so. In this way, the cycle of disadvantage is perpetuated.

Literacy, care, respect and recognition

NLS have argued persuasively that literacy processes and events, and those who participate in them, cannot be viewed separately from the culture in which they are situated. Literacy is not economically or politically neutral in that it reflects and expresses socio-economic and power relations and their differential impact on the learning chances of individuals and groups. So also literacy is bound up in the cultural hierarchies, contexts, behaviours, traditions and values within which language evolves, and meaning is expressed, construed and negotiated. The nature of different literacy events also mirrors and forms a part of the normative weights and balances of recognition, value and respect that permeate society. Gender, sexuality, race, ethnicity, age, class, and other aspects of identity are implicated in determining by whom culture is named, and whose experience and identity is sidelined, devalued or discarded as not meriting equal respect and recognition. Those who are culturally oppressed, who belong to 'othered', less cared about groups, tend also to be less well resourced and represented. This combination of factors can result in educational disadvantage and unmet literacy needs that have cultural causes as well as consequences.

Literacy and being 'other'

Illiteracy is both a cause and a consequence of being perceived as 'other' (Stuart and Thompson, 1995). Adult literacy narratives repeatedly articulate the reality of those whose care-less school experience impacts on their adult life and that of their children.

> I was left-handed and I remember that feeling of being made to write with my right hand. I think it had an awful effect on me—a terrible effect. It ruined my self-confidence too. It made me understand a lot about people being persecuted for whatever it is. I was saying—why is she treating me different because I'm left-handed? Such a stupid, stupid thing—to me it was persecution. I'm going to make you like everybody else in the class.

Even when my children started school and I brought them up—the smell of the school and the whole atmosphere just brought me back there. And maybe something goes wrong and you have to go and face the headmaster. You are an adult. You are in charge of your life but at the same time this is the headmaster and you have this thing in your head from years ago. That affects your relationship for your children and all.

(Northern Ireland Civic Forum, 2002: 43)

Figure 3.3: Respect and recognition *in the dynamic cycle of learning care*

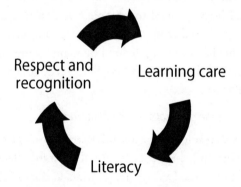

Many adults' memories of school recall teachers' differential expectations of achievement, behaviour and attitudes towards those whose parents had prestige and status in the community and those whose primary carers were poor, lone parents, unemployed or otherwise perceived to be of less value. This contributed to a sense of alienation, early school leaving and underachievement in literacy and learning in general. In later life, the same misrecognition leaves a legacy of self-depreciation and a reluctance to believe that learning literacy is even a possibility. Even the most rudimentary self-care is withheld (Bailey and Coleman, 1998).

Until relatively recently, those with particular learning care needs, those with learning difficulties or disabilities and those whose learning pace or style differed from the perceived norm were educationally sidelined. Little or no effort was made to discover appropriate ways to meet their diverse literacy learning needs. Consequentially, the identity of those with unmet literacy needs is representative of groups to which Baker *et al.*, (2004:154) refer as the 'culturally marginal'. Not only are minority cultural needs discounted but also positive images of them are absent in learning materials and their unequal position thereby reinforced and reproduced. At the same time as being failed by the education system, those who are thus rendered invisible, who are effaced from what is respected and valued, internalise their lack of worth and learn to fail.

As well as being part of the culture of any society, proficiency in language and literacy are also the vehicle through which much cultural activity is carried (Gramsci, 1971; 1995). Opportunities to access and participate in these events and practices are restricted for those without language competence. Creativity is denied, important aspects of self-actualisation stunted and group expression restricted and silenced for those who are othered by the text-dominated culture (Askew and Carnell, 1998; Boal, 2000). Throughout history, powerful groups have monopolised literacy's vital mnemonic function to ensure that written records present a preferred truth and other voices and identities go unheard and unheeded. This has been highlighted by many groups including women (Ward, 1983) working class people (O'Neill, 1992; 2000) and people of colour (hooks, 1989, 2000).

The other side of care: the cultural stigma of illiteracy

Unmet literacy needs result in negative and destructive emotions of fear, anxiety, guilt, anger, despair and their consequential harmful affect experienced as humiliation and internalised as self-deprecation. Giddens (1994) argued that this internalised impact of structural inequalities on self-esteem acts as a self-activated exclusionary mechanism. Such evidence is present in literacy students' narratives about childhood and learning experiences. They are also theorised in studies into the whole area of *stigma*.

With its origins in the physical marking out of those deemed shameful in ancient Greek society, *stigma* is used as a metaphor for the perceived cause of a flawed or spoiled identity. In effect, a stigma is really about a relationship between expected and actual social identity. The discrepancy is linked to an attribute (or lack) that obtrudes other characteristics and renders the bearer socially stereotyped, devalued, marginalised and prey to discrimination and unequal treatment. Stigma and discrimination are intricately interlinked (Goffman, 1963; Lemert and Branaman, 1997; Fine and Smith, 2000) and the causes of shameful differentness change with time and evolving social judgements of what is acceptable. Stigmas are therefore socially constructed and similarly can be socially dismantled.

As has been established in Chapter two, having unmet literacy needs has become increasingly stigmatised with the spread of universal free education. So it is increasingly associated with degradation, lack of esteem, respect and value of the individuals and groups affected. Blame and negativity attaches to the learner whom the system has failed rather than to the structures that perform unevenly across the groups to which they have an equal responsibility (Field, 2000; 2002). We live in a culture that confers high esteem on the uses of literacy but fails to ensure that this basic currency is equally accessible to all citizens. It then invests relatively little in remedying its own failure.

Unmet literacy needs are degrading in that an individual or group are denied access to a vital tool for full participation in everyday life, for self-fulfilment, well-being and access to all forms of capital (Bourdieu, 1986). The state through its unequal delivery of education therefore fails in its duty of care to equally respect those affected citizens. Additionally, the process of *becoming illiterate* that is largely synonymous with early schooling is fraught with narratives of abuse, disrespect, abasement and destruction of self-confidence. The immediate outcome causes misery throughout the schooling process. The longer-term consequences extend this injustice, and often deep psychological damage throughout many aspects of adulthood (Bailey and Coleman, 1998; Goffman, 1963; Owens, 2000).

Goffman (1963) cites illiteracy as one of a range of stigmatising factors that lead to a recognisable pattern of behaviours. Although by no means universal, a typical feature of stigmatisation is avoidance of contact with 'normals'. Many of those with literacy needs avoid social situations liable to expose them and live in a tortuous state of anxiety and tension because of the fragility of their concealment. Goffman's extensive study of stigmatised persons describes a harmful absence of 'the salutary feedback of daily social intercourse with others' that in the case of the adult with literacy needs means lack of equal access to personal relationships, solidarity and community inclusion. Internalised prejudice can result in self-loathing, isolation and depression (Goffman, 1963: 19).

In a more positive vein, many of those faced with managing a literacy-linked spoiled identity, develop adeptness in coping with the practical daily challenges of life in a text-based, knowledge society and in sustaining carefully selected networks of support and solidary friendships (Ibid: 31). When, as with illiteracy, a stigma is invisible, a person becomes discreditable rather than discredited and the fairly constant pressure of choices about passing, and the uncertainty of rejection or acceptance, is ever-present in the formation and maintenance of all types of relationship (ibid: 57). The stress extends beyond the individuals directly affected to those intimates (often children) who are required to collude in the concealment. An oppressive and burdensome division inevitably builds between the lifeworld inhabited by those who know the secret and those who do not.

Affective literacy paradigms

With states experiencing ongoing reluctance from adults to engage in mainstream adult literacy provision, increasing attention is being given to a new affective paradigm that links literacy into existing relationships of trust. At the same time, the focus is diverted away from state duties of learning care and responsibility of the education system to ensure equal literacy outcomes for all. This paradigmatic shift is true of Workplace Literacy that relies on Trade Union, solidary bonds to engage reluctant learners (Payne, 2001; Shelley, 2005). It is the basis of community-based literacy that tries to attract people into learning near home, in a familiar environment and in the company of trusted neighbours and associates (Feeley, 2001). In its most primary form, the affective paradigm draws on family relationships.

By far the most prevalent example of the new affective literacy paradigm is that of family literacy where *'parents'* are cast as pedagogues but in reality it is primarily the mother who is pressured to become literacy teacher for her children. Recent 'photovoice' research conversations with disadvantaged parents about their understandings of family literacy revealed an awareness of the sometimes synonymous nature of early literacy and primary care (Hegarty and Feeley, 2010: 51).

> Actually when I am doing homework with the young fellow he is kind of sitting up and kind of leaning against me as if to say I am well supported here. He feels safe. So I think love should go in there. When they come in from school they come to me for a hug and the same before they leave in the morning. That is their support. (Mother aged 42 with four children)

This new duty adds to the already complex nature of parenting, particularly for women who have had difficult childhoods themselves and who live, as do many women and girls, with the reality or legacy of violence in their adult life (Horsman, 2000; 2004). Horsman argues that the moral imperative to be literacy tutor to her children can bring competing priorities into play and arouse conflicts for mothers who are already struggling to prioritise their own learning needs.

Central in these dominant mothering discourses are assumptions about the 'normal' family where the mother is present as nurturer and literacy tutor and ultimately held responsible for the child's success in public education. Smythe and Isserlis (2003) argue that such discourses create gendered, cultural inequalities in literacy care labour where notions of the ideal mother fail to reflect the harsh reality of many women's lives. They cite Jane Mace's (1998) historical study of the links between mothering and literacy to suggest that the relatively recent additional role of teacher is arbitrary and rooted more in a socio-economic agenda than in the natural role of mother. Maces' study of the late nineteenth and early twentieth centuries shows how women with little access to literacy in their own lives, nonetheless reared literate children. Their contribution was to establish a solid affective base that enabled literacy learning in school rather than being able themselves to directly address literacy issues. This suggests that nurture and care are indeed pivotal in supporting literacy development.

Nussbaum (2000) also identifies the family as the key social institution where anything above basic levels of love and care can be attained but the imprint of these childhood experiences is not always predictable. Studies of intergenerational continuity in parenting and attachment patterns suggest that it is how childhood experience is construed, rather than the objective facts, that determine the likelihood of pattern rigidity (Goldberg, 2000; Gross, 2001). This in turn goes some way to explaining different outcomes for siblings from the same family and inmates of care institutions with similar childhood experiences of nurture (or lack of it). It also justifies calls for increased resourcing of parents in disadvantaged circumstances and the provision of effective counselling support for those surviving traumatic and affectively damaging childhoods (Herman, 1997).

Generational learning patterns

Teaching and learning are relational activities and function around a complex web of relationships and connections. For a child, the caring relationship with parents and the informal learning that takes place in the family are vital foundations for other, later learning activities. Attitudes are developed and a sense of self is rooted in the very early years before formal schooling begins (Barton, 2007). Parents' own negative experience of learning, in addition to shaping the course of their own life chances, will be key in determining the future of subsequent generations. An adult with unhappy memories of school may determine that this will not be repeated in her own child's life and struggle for this to be the case. The opposite may equally be true and someone who has been damaged by unpleasant school events may feel powerless in supporting their child's transition into formal schooling and their future learning (O'Brien, 2005; Reay, 2000; Standing, 1999). The determinants of this dynamic are complex and unpredictable but the potential for harm is clearly located in learning structures and not in the badly-served citizens and groups. By the time the parents' relationship to the school (Reay, 1998), pupil–teacher and pupil–pupil relations all become significant, many suggest that the die is already definitively cast for the new generation of learner (Lee and Burkham, 2002; Northern Ireland Civic Forum, 2002).

Literacy, care and relationships of power

Inequalities of power are interwoven with other inequalities of respect and recognition and particularly economic inequalities. Ann Phillips (1999) has illustrated how the poverty, disrespect and misrecognition of some individuals and groups effectively restrict their use of power, even though equality of worth is widely proclaimed. Education has a pivotal role in perpetuating and challenging inequalities that are not only ingrained in educational structures but also in the texts used throughout the curriculum (Apple 1993a; 1993b). Power-based learning care inequalities have their roots in political structures that legitimate some voices and silence others (Lynch and O'Neill, 1994). The hierarchical relationships that the educational system sanctions and indeed fosters are visible in a literacy curriculum that reflects wider power agendas and squeezes out the vernacular literacy needs of less powerful groups. All learning is rife with power and literacy policies, practice, processes and events are constantly in motion to control, reproduce and only occasionally to challenge the status quo (Freire and Macedo, 1987; Powell, 1999). The solidary, power-sharing relationships that are a feature of much adult literacy practice are an indication of the potential for individual and even group change within the literacy movement (Searle, 1975; 1998). At the same time, the low status of literacy work within the field of education means that its proponents are themselves relatively powerless alongside more influential disciplines. In many countries this hierarchy of knowledge is reflected in rates of tutor pay where literacy is paid at the lowest grade.

The acquisition of literacy and its uses reflect these patterns of power in wider society where those who are powerless are less cared *about* and less cared *for* both at a systemic and micro level in the education structure. If educational equality were an honest rather than rhetorical priority then this would be reflected in levels of investment and the targeting of concern at those who do not now acquire the basic level of literacy from years of compulsory schooling. Even in the Irish boom years adult literacy was the most poorly funded area of education and this was symptomatic of how state care-lessness allowed productivity power to take priority over individual and community well-being.

A history of power and control

Chapter two described the way that literacy has historically been the accessory of those in the economic, cultural and political élite. Possession of the information contained in the written word has always been synonymous with power and supremacy. At the same time, not having literacy may be associated with a sense of relative powerlessness, underdevelopment and inadequacy in text related tasks. The term *illiterate* can be used abusively to insult and wound and denote emotions of disrespect and disgust.

The narratives of adults whose literacy capabilities remain unrealised are filled with accounts of abuses and misuses of power. Adult literacy students cite incidences of violence against them as children in and outside the classroom, paralysing authoritarian school structures that streamed and labelled them and dismissed their potential. They describe oppressive relationships with some teachers (Bailey and Coleman, 1998; Northern Ireland Civic Forum, 2002). These individuals are in no doubt about the resultant inequalities in learning care that they experienced although their voices are rarely taken into account (Lynch and O'Neill, 1994; O'Neill, 1992).

Figure 3.4: Power *in the dynamic cycle of learning care*

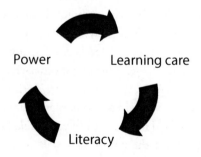

What Gardner (1993; 1999) described as an '*IQ way of thinking*' and measuring has thwarted the development of diverse capabilities for generations (Goleman, 1996:38). In the same way, the notion of *functional literacy* is wielding similar constraining power over the field of adult literacy. Narrow notions of what it means to be literate and to *function* as an obedient worker and consumer pervade dominant literacy discourse and underpin National Literacy Tests and the Literacy Core Curriculum in the UK and elsewhere (Street, 2011).

Fawns and Ivanic (2001) illustrate how the practice of form filling epitomises this process of social regulation and discipline in an information driven world. Forms provoke emotions of frustration and anxiety even in those with confidence in literacy. Such bureaucratic, mechanistic forms of literacy are increasingly the focus of courses aimed at providing adults with the skills necessary to *function* in today's world. Limiting the expectations of so many at a functional level of literacy in today's knowledge society is oppressive and disempowering. It only takes care of the interests of those who require us to decode and encode a very limited range of messages. It does not allow for the literacy needs of those who may want to reflect, question, create, criticise or variously be part of a democratic process that considers change desirable and possible (Powell, 1999). The disproportionate favour now being extended to those who are already privileged in society can only be comprehensively tackled at a structural level and this is unlikely to be undertaken by those that the system now privileges (Lynch, 1999: 287-309; Lynch and Baker, 2005).

The other side of care: Illiteracy as social harm

Equity suggests that literacy should be prioritised as one of the most basic building blocks for other formal and informal learning and for full participation in everyday life. Given the inequalities between families, the primary responsibility for facilitating the acquisition of literacy must lie with the state through the education system. Conversely, the inability to ensure all citizens with this capability achieve the most basic levels of education amounts to failure in a duty of care at a structural level. This might otherwise be described as *social harm* and benefit from attention from such a perspective (Hillyard *et al.*, 2004).

With a primary focus in the field of criminology but nonetheless interesting for its application to the field of literacy, Hillyard *et al.*, (2004) argue for a new discipline organised around the notion of *social harm*. They contend that it is without sense or veracity to separate out harms that are currently socially construed as criminal from other harms that affect peoples' lives and life chances. Such a limited view of criminality leads to neglect of all the other harmful events, experiences and unequal social structures that have significant and often injurious impact on everyday existence. A social harm perspective (also known as Zemiology or zemiotics from the Greek *zemia* meaning harm) has greater social justice as its impetus and understands much that it sees as harm as 'the social wreckage of neo-liberal globalisation' (Hillyard *et al.*, 2004: 3). The proponents of zemiology suggest that harm may be physical, economic/financial, emotional and psychological and related to cultural safety.

In the related category of 'state harm', Tony Ward describes as 'especially serious harm' the failure by the state to provide 'sufficient education… to enable one to play a part in the life of ones society' (Ward, 2004: 85). It is arguably the case that just such isolation and exclusion is the consequential reality for many adults and groups with unmet literacy needs. In a similar vein, making a specific link between literacy as a capability and 'compassion in public life', Nussbaum refers to literacy as a most basic expectation for all citizens.

> … society ought to guarantee its citizens a threshold level of … adequate
> education, including but by no means limited to, literacy.
>
> (Nussbaum, 2001: 416-417)

Illiteracy, like the distribution of various other harms, mirrors patterns strongly linked to areas of disadvantage and inequality and in this regard the notion of a harmed community, or a harmed community of interest has value and significance for further exploration.

Illiteracy as a violation of rights

Jamil Salmi (2004: 55-66) argues that though they fall short of direct physical violence, many aspects of state neglect can be harmful to individuals and groups. This is true both in the immediate and long-term as the shadow of unmet literacy needs projects its influence ever more darkly into adulthood. In this sense, illiteracy becomes a factor that puts a person's physical or psychological well-being directly under threat and thereby may be understood as an act of violation. By failing to provide equal protection against poverty, hunger, disease and accidents, unmet literacy needs become acts of violation 'by omission.' By potentially restricting fundamental civil, political and social rights, unmet literacy needs are a form of repression; and by denying a person the right to equal psychological, emotional, cultural and intellectual integrity, unmet literacy needs constitute a form of alienation (Salmi, 2004: 55-66). Indirect, repressive and alienating violations of rights as described by Salmi mirror the less emotionally stated contexts of resource, political and cultural inequality (Baker *et al.*, 2004) and give a sense of the complicated consequential impacts unmet literacy needs may produce.

State duty of care

A social harm perspective (Hillyard *et al.*, 2004), like an equality of condition perspective (Lynch and Baker, 2005), would locate the remedial imperative for unmet literacy needs within the area of state priorities of policy and expenditure. It would situate the root cause of persistent poor literacy performance in structural political inequalities rather than as is currently implied, that 'the difficulty' begins and ends with certain problematic (rather than harmed) individuals and groups. This would not be popular, as it would identify the state as the real source of harm and those who are educationally disadvantaged as victims of state neglect. While dominant discourses invest considerable effort in maintaining a focus on failing schools, falling standards, dysfunctional families, communities and identities, this deficit manner of framing literacy issues obfuscates the real root cause of educational inequalities and the locus of power and responsibility to bring about change.

The question of responsibility is interesting. If, as Zemiology suggests, murders in the UK are increasingly concentrated in areas of extreme poverty, does responsibility lie solely with the disadvantaged individual killer or with state failure to eradicate the causal poverty in which s/he lives and acts (Dorling, 2004:)? Can a parent who has not received adequate basic education be held responsible for her children's poor educational outcomes? A social harm stance implies the need to politicise and democratise the business of learning care and keep the impetus for progress where the power of agency (and funding) really lie—in the hands of the state.

The view of schooling as harmful is not new. The issue is repeatedly highlighted in the personal history narratives of adult literacy learners and in decades of research in schools (Hannan and Shorthall, 1991; Lynch and Lodge, 2002; Lyons *et al.*, 2003; Russell, 2011). Roy Parker also questions the 'emotional damage wrought by unsympathetic styles of teaching and bullying at school' and the 'emotional abuse' of children caused by unnecessary suffering in insensitive institutional care or penal establishments (Parker, 2004: 239). This serves as a reminder that the continuum of affective inequality in relation to literacy learning and use is long, and the experiences of individuals and groups far from homogeneous.

The often-neglected emotional work that takes place in education becomes increasingly relevant when put in the context of altering patterns of generational, traumatic childhood experiences. Lynch and Lodge (2002) cite extensive evidence from research that has been carried out *with* young people, rather than *on* them, that indicates that schools do in fact cause harm to young learners. This is attributed to the impact of an authoritarian, class-bound, competitive ethos and associated practices of many schools. It is due in particular to the ways in which these regimes of control are interpreted and enacted by those involved in teacher training and by individual tutors themselves. Research in secondary schools challenges the dominant cognitive (and cultural) analyses and proposes that the importance of the affective be reconsidered and the specifics of equality of care become the subject of future educational programmes and empirical educational studies (Lynch and Baker, 2005; Lynch and Lodge, 2002:11-13; McClave, 2005). Bringing feminist and Freirean discourse into dialogue, Maeve O'Brien (2011: 33) calls for the process of care-full education to begin with 'teachers as educarers', and by implication their educators. She identifies the need to engage in critical reflection about the reality of being involved in the pursuit of an education for humanisation. As a form of resistance against the productivity model of education, this may well be a good place to begin.

Literacy and relationships of solidarity

Solidarity is a form of power that is achieved when we collectivise or pool forces in order to act in concert around an issue (Allen, 1999). In psychological terms solidarity, or group cohesion, satisfies fundamental and very different care needs. On the one hand solidary behaviour can be the result of empathetic emotions like sympathy, compassion and tenderness that result in a type of 'we-ness' and shared purpose. On the other hand, self-oriented emotions of discomfort, anxiety and upset can lead people to bond together in a desire to reduce their own distress (Gross, 2001: 433-455; Hogg and Vaughan, 1998; Piliavin *et al.*, 1981). Examples of both these diverse ends of the solidary continuum can be found in adult literacy work.

Exclusion from a peer group at school for reasons of perceived difference, bullying or protracted absence can all result in unmet literacy needs. In the same way a sense of belonging and the well-being that accompanies it can facilitate learning and make schooling an enjoyable and successful experience. Those who do not grasp literacy at school and who make the brave step back into learning often discover an energising feeling of solidarity from the power-sharing experience of learning in an adult group. There is a sense of shared struggle in literacy work not just for learners but also for tutors and organisers whose work is often undervalued and marginalised in the adult education sector.

For the most part, unmet adult literacy needs denote and ensure relative powerlessness and an absence of learning care, in a predominantly literate society. Disadvantaged individuals and groups are less cared about in an education system that, at all levels of learning, privileges the economically and socially powerful. Unmet literacy needs imply that individual learning potential has not been identified and tapped and that sufficient care has not been taken to find methods and approaches to match diverse learning needs.

Where adults are able to speak for themselves and ask for appropriate literacy support, these power inequalities can be dismantled and replaced by a solidary, power-sharing second chance to learn. The capacity to exercise this power is inextricably linked to other equalities of respect and recognition, and economic equality in particular.

Conclusion

Pivotal learning care inequalities, those that reside in the affective domain, are causally and consequentially linked to issues of resources, power and social status. Where learning care is constrained by other inequalities, the proposition is that unmet literacy needs can result and patterns and cycles of inequality and injustice are replicated and reproduced. Many of those individuals and groups who are denied love, care and solidarity by unequal social structures are also those who may miss out on literacy.

A meritocratic education system that is not accompanied by equality of condition perpetuates and constantly revitalises the educational privilege of those who are better off. The absence of early years' provision and quality childcare for working parents means that a substantial class-based learning gap is already in place before primary schooling begins. This does not mean, as Heckman and Masterov (2004) suggest, that economically disadvantaged parents care less about their children. Rather it indicates that they have less financial, material, cultural, temporal and corporal resources to draw upon in carrying out an increasingly demanding learning support role.

Literacy is fundamentally relational and those whose full language capabilities are impaired are consequentially weakened in the extent to which they can fully participate in societal structures and pursue their economic, political and cultural goals in life. They are curtailed in their social involvement and the resources they can deploy in relationships of solidarity and intimacy. The state's failure in its duty of care to provide basic education for all citizens is harmful not only in the immediate unsuccessful experience of learning but also in the long-term influence it wields over the lives and communities of those affected, as well as their dependants. Further evidence of the links between care and other aspects of equality are explored now through the data.

Chapter 4

Lessons about resourcing learning care:
Literacy and the affective/resource interface

> Money is not everything but it does help if you can use it to educate your
> kids. I know that most people who are on the bread line try and look after
> the kids and find it very hard and their kids are missing out. So money
> is important.   (Liam)

This is the first of three findings chapters in which the words of the research
participants are central to illustrating the different contexts of in/equality
described in the equality framework in discussed in chapter two. Here, the
interface between resources and care is explored through the data in relation
to respondents' early and adult literacy learning experience. Resources are
understood not just in terms of financial assets but also the whole broader
portfolio of capitals that underwrite literacy learning. Learning care is confirmed
in the data as a form of care-related labour that required a range of human
and material resources. These included presence, time and effort on the part
of primary caregivers as well as teachers' professional competence in terms of
attitude, skills and knowledge about how literacy learning works. Deficits in all
aspects of such resources were shown to have impacted on the quality of learning
care available to individuals in industrial schools and their subsequent literacy
outcomes. So, often through their absence, we learn about the resources that
caregivers need in order to provide effective learning care.

Resources are undoubtedly a major enabling factor in the amount and
consistency of care and learning care that can be given in any learning context.
Although almost all of the respondents in this study were from impoverished
families, it is important to clarify that being poor or working class should by
no means be seen as synonymous with caring less about one's children. Rather,
as the quote above articulates, those whose stock of capitals was low were
unequally placed to provide the learning care they would like their children to
receive. Disadvantage in the resources that enable care and its *learning care labour*
had a marked effect on the capacity of individuals and groups in this study to
reap the benefits of education. The literature describes how those who access

only impoverished learning support, whether in the public or private sphere, cannot match the learning outcomes of those to whom economic and capital-rich privilege is readily available (Clancy, 2001; Daly and Leonard, 2002; Lynch, 1999). Figures for university access for example show that less well-off people are still only fractionally represented in comparison to others (Gregory and Williams, 2004; Reay *et al.*, 2010). At the extreme end of the care continuum, those for whom care and learning care labour was poorly or negatively resourced were unequally challenged to achieve and retain even basic levels of literacy.

Inevitably this educational injustice impacts on subsequent adult life prospects and on the social and economic fortune of future generations. An affective-resource cycle was recognised in the Irish State's definition of the 'psychological injury' and 'loss of opportunity' suffered by children from industrial schools where they cited 'underachievement in literacy and having to refuse employment opportunity or promotion because of illiteracy' as a direct consequence of institutional abuse (Residential Institutions Redress Board (RIRB), second edition 2004). This again begs the question, raised throughout this text, as to what the state's corresponding position should be in relation to all those who are, to this day, similarly disadvantaged by structural inequalities in general and specifically in the education system (Ward, 2004).

Making a poor mouth

Resource inequality was both a primary cause and subsequently a consequence of institutionalisation. Institutions were financially resourced by the state and some evidence suggests that these resources were inadequate for the task. In a report to the Department of Education and Skills (DES) by the Compensation Advisory Committee (2002:11) the opinion was stated that the state failed in its duty to properly regulate industrial schools and to pay adequate capitation grants. The report cites Kennedy:

> The managers in charge of schools were faced with the task of running institutions on a totally inadequate financial provision and were forced to supplement their incomes by whatever means possible to enable their work to continue … What was worse was that the services available to the children were, of necessity, of a rather limited nature. When the cost of necessities had been deducted there was little if any left over for provision of those extra compensatory facilities which are considered necessary for

the rehabilitation of deprived children … no grants were made available
for maintenance, renovation or modernisation of premises.

Kennedy Report (1970: 13, 28 & 29)

Religious orders repeatedly claimed that the state did not provide adequately
for the number of children who ended up in their custody and this issue
continues to be disputed. Raftery and O'Sullivan (1999) refuted attempts to cite
inadequate resource factors as an explanation and excuse for the paucity of care
that was given to residents in industrial schools. A three-part TV series *States
of Fear*[13] produced documentary evidence that the accounts of some industrial
schools showed substantial surpluses for periods when they were claiming to
be under-resourced.

For whatever reason, it remains clear from the narratives that the care survivors
received in every aspect of their lives was impoverished and that the ultimate
resource responsibility for this lay with the state into whose safekeeping children
had been taken.

> There are a lot of [literacy] problems and the anger is actually that, "they
> were meant to care for me. They were meant to make things better; they
> were given the responsibility to care for me because my family couldn't
> do it, or weren't doing it or were told not to do it and they just made
> matters worse".   *Centre worker*

Basic resource needs

In the first instance, human and material resources were key to admission to
residential care. The collapse of a family unit might have resulted from poverty,
destitution, homelessness, lone-parenthood, death of a parent or the breakdown
in a marital relationship. When the combined resource and affective burden
became prohibitive and no adequate state welfare safety net existed, institutional
care was often the imposed or reluctantly chosen, alternative. Residency in an
industrial school was presented as ensuring the satisfaction of minimum care
needs and educational provision but this is now acknowledged not to have been
the case in practice (Department of Education and Skills, 2002; Shield, 2006).
Although often taken from families because of resource difficulties, those in

13. These programmes were shown on Radio Telifís Eireann (RTE) on 15, 22 and 29
    July, 2003.

the proxy care of the state, reported deprivation even of the most rudimentary kind. These neglects impacted on learning in childhood and continued to cast long shadows over attempts at learning in adulthood.

Need for space and air

Even at the most fundamental level, resources were limited. The Compensation Advisory Committee (Department of Education and Skills, 2002) acknowledged the prevalence of agoraphobia, claustrophobia and panic states amongst survivors. This was attributed to the closed nature of institutions and, in particular, a long-term effect of sexual abuse.

> I would have always hated school. I found it very claustrophobic you know. I don't like being in enclosed spaces, you know, like in big groups and the like. *Bill*

A sense of claustrophobia is commonly described amongst survivors. One woman who spent her entire childhood in care told me she was now only really at peace when out of doors. Another woman who spent ten years in care between the ages of seven and seventeen has carried the stifling, physical sense of repression throughout her adult life:

> But even now when I wake up I have to put my head out the window. I feel the need for air (pause) fresh air all the time. And it is to do with the suffocation. *Carol*

Carol described how as a child she was obliged by older girls to act as a hot-water bottle. She had to take up her position under the covers at the bottom of the bed and remain there until the older girl went to bed and used Carol to warm her feet.

A counsellor of survivors of institutional abuse confirmed that this claustrophobia was a common issue raised by his clients during therapy. I myself noted that survivors liked to sit where they could see the door and literacy tutors working with them had learned that doors needed to be left open for adult learners to feel at ease. Writing from a psychotherapeutic perspective, Paul Shield suggests that:

Children became recipients of often malignant, at times toxic, care, in institutions in which, due to the absence of knowledgeable care, the primary task developed in an 'unthinking' way and came to take on the claustrophobic and perverse features of the claustrum.[14]

(Shield, 2006: 26)

The fear of enclosure and its manifestation in frequent panic attacks and a need for airy spaces also impeded survivors in their long pursuit of literacy.

I felt strange going into a one-to-one at first. It was like (pause) when you go into see somebody in one-to-one like and (pause) I'd often say 'will I ever get out of here?' And like when I was in one-to-one when the door was closed I thought they were going to lock it because if they locked that door I would have panicked. I'd have to get out real quick. I probably would have had to kick the door real quick.   *Jennifer*

Food and drink

Many respondents had been hungry in their family situations and some talked of stealing food so as not to go hungry. In families, food meant love and care and a mother was 'good' who managed or even tried to put food on the table. Even in the poorest homes, children felt that at least a caring adult arbitrated the burden of providing for basic needs.

With separation and particularly with abandonment, accessing food and water to survive became primal acts without the garnish of affection. Bill told me he was placed in care by court order at the age of six along with three brothers aged two, four and eight. He began the two-day journey from home to his new place of care in good spirits, excited about being in a car for the first time in his life. The next day he and his older brother were left in one institution and his younger siblings were taken off to the nuns. These explanations were only pieced together years afterwards. He eventually arrived in a large refectory, hungry and mesmerised by the strangeness of everything. He remembered feeling particularly hungry because the hospital where he had slept en route the previous night had offered only unfamiliar and unpalatable fare. He then

14. The claustrum refers to the physical and symbolic boundary between the internal and external world, usually in relation to religious buildings where the 'cloister' marked the line that lay people could not pass.

described his first experience of industrial school life and the stark message it communicated to him, at age six, about the absence of a primary carer in his life and the monumental task of survival.

> Yeah I was starving. But it was packed. I seen all these kids. It struck me and from then on it struck me, from now on Bill you are looking after yourself. By the time grace before meals was said every piece of food that was on the tables was gone. So I was still starving and that was another day without food. But it was that early on that I knew this wasn't something small. This was big. This was something that was going to affect my life big time.   *Bill*

Even something as simple as a drink of water became a source of deprivation and anxiety. A woman related how she covertly accessed water in the institution.

> If you wanted a drink of anything you went to the toilet and you got a drink of water there. There weren't taps knocking about or these things here where you get fresh water. There was nothing like that. You went to the loo and you got it out of the cistern if you were lucky, but more often out of the toilet bowl because the cistern would have made a noise. *Brenda*

These primary deprivations kept learning literacy a low priority. Hunger, combined and associated with the absence of affection placed major barriers in the way of absorbing and processing new information. Unrequited basic care needs and fear of punishment dominated children's horizons and many were passive and unaware of the long-term benefits of education. This was a familiar pattern for a psychologist employed by the state to prepare reports on survivors attending the Redress Board.

> You can't learn if you are shut down. You live day to day. A lot of the people who came in here would say that they could only think forward until their next meal or until they met the person that they most feared in the institution. There was no sense of 'I am going to learn so I can have a better life when I get out of here'. It was just day-to-day survival really for a lot of the people that I saw. Certainly the physical environment meant they were often hungry and cold. They were losing out on that just physical ability to be comfortable in your skin. And a lot of them were

just very, very lonely. And again it is no surprise that sense of loneliness and 'I am not worth it so there is no point'. Somebody else has my life in their control, so what is the point? There is a kind of hopelessness about it.   *Psychologist*

Security and attachment

Black American writer and educator, bell hooks (1997) talks about the need for a secure 'homeplace' where learners find their sense of self-assurance before moving confidently into the stranger environments with which life presents them. This learning version of attachment theory suggests that early learning relationships and environments establish patterns and coping strategies for times to come. Feeling safe and secure, experiencing the benign routine that facilitates the development of stable, well-adjusted early learners was an understanding that often came only in later life.

> Well I think it is very different for my granddaughter. When she picked up a book and was able to read it, I was so happy. You know? And it also made me feel (breaks down crying) what I would have been... with a normal (pause) let us put it this way. That is the kind of family I would have liked to come from.   *Jane*

> I see my own sister with her children and like I see how (pause) the playroom is full of books and the child is learning. He is only five and he is reading already and you can see the difference in the child. I look at him and see that is how life should have been for me.   *Bob*

Survivors missed out on those very basics of environmental and emotional stability. Often they were taken without explanation from home and familial connections to an institution where there was no caring adult figure and home became a punishing regime that was both physically and emotionally insecure.

Paul's story is a sequence of affective deprivations, the consequences of which have a constant impact. Aged seventy-four, he has learned literacy in the past five years. When his father left the family they went to the County Home or Poor House. After the loss of a child his mother suffered a mental breakdown. He was six when he went into care at which point he was told that everyone belonging to him was dead. This was untrue and he was subsequently reunited with his mother and some of his siblings when he was sixteen. He went to England with his brother and earned his living as a groundsman for a local council. He evaded reading and writing by relying on literate friends and was promoted to a senior position because of his skills and reliability. He married late in life because he had been warned in school against the dangers of associating with women, who were the 'personification of evil'. When his wife died he came back to Ireland and made three attempts on his life before finding solidary support in the Lighthouse Centre. Despite all of this he is a jovial, communicative man who tells his story easily. Through counselling, he is just learning to name his emotional world and confront the painful revelations that accompany this knowledge.

> Paul told me the other day about being on the Luas[15] and a man got up and he had his arm around his little boy, his son, and he was asking him something and he was explaining it to him like about the wires or something. And he said "I now know that what I was when I looked at them was jealous. I didn't know about those feelings and what they were. I was jealous because nobody ever put their arm around me, you know, and explained things to me".   *Centre Worker*

As children in the institutions survivors could either make comparisons with memories of home life or they weighed their lot against that of other children. They observed that learning literacy seemed easier for those with a safe homeplace.

> I lived at home with them [parents] until I was five and that is hugely influential because my sister was two [going into care] and you can see the three years that I got that she didn't get. The extra three years of nurturing from your own parent as opposed to my sister who was literally a baby going into care. She hadn't got the same foundation as I had as I would have had five solid years and she would have had only two. Even a little bit of encouragement that I got stood to me.   *Brenda*

Kevin had been at home until he was seven and could clearly name the role of primary care relationships in learning.

15. Dublin's Light Rail Tram System

The way I look at it is that some people did well because they were connected with their families outside. They had their families to support them. They were able to concentrate better. Their thinking was different. People that did well at the school had their families looking after them. While they went home to their families, I was going back to a regime. They were going back to their families. It was very different. They would be helped. We wouldn't be helped. *Kevin*

Bob, now forty-one, spent his early childhood from the age of six in an industrial school and as a young teenager moved into a 'family unit'. He was safe in neither place. He was emotionally and sexually abused in both establishments and had deep psychological issues that make learning literacy, even as an adult, extremely difficult.

I would have been a very emotionally disturbed child living there anyhow. It wasn't a nice place to be as a child and you couldn't possibly have learnt or reached your potential there. *Bob*

Comfortless and shaped by insecurity, the industrial school was devoid of the care that humanises through fostering and building good relationships. Classrooms were places of fear and the preoccupation of children within them was to avoid beating and humiliation.

I didn't like the school there. I hated it. There was a terrible tense atmosphere. And like you would be looking at them to see if they were in a bad mood. There was always somebody getting a right beating. And you were tense all through the class and afraid. If you got something to do you would be scared. I didn't like it—it was too tense. *Kevin*

Others described a sensation of unease in relation to finding themselves in a strange place from which they needed to be rescued.

I could see, even as a child I could see that there was something wrong there; that I shouldn't have been in this position. *Kevin*

When you talk to children about being taken away from home they talk a lot about rescue—you know their stories are always along the lines of

… they are the princess or the prince in the tower waiting for somebody
to come and rescue them and they are not being rescued. Something goes
wrong with the rescue and you can see that feeling persists with some of
the adults as well.   *Centre worker*

A safe and caring learning environment suggests a context where a minimum
of security and appropriate resources are assured to everyone irrespective of
other inequalities. This is so that a learner is confident in the starting point
from which they begin to process new information. Those for whom nothing
was fixed and certain, physically, materially or emotionally, operated from a
negative, care-less base position.

Bedwetting and sleep

Not surprisingly, the distress engendered by hunger, fear, separation from family
and an absence of any form of affective relief became magnified in the darkness
of night and many children wet the bed. Wetting the bed in turn lead to lack of
sleep as children were wakened frequently during the night and taken to the toilet.
The threat of punishment for such misdemeanours was ever present exacerbated
by name-calling and a range of other debasing practices. 'Wet the beds' were
made to stand all night in corridors wrapped in their wet sheet. They then had
to wash the sheet the next morning as further punishment on top of physical
chastisement. In one establishment, the names of bedwetters were also placed
in a book that was read aloud each morning causing further public humiliation.

Both male and female respondents classified bedwetting as a major factor that
impaired learning. Not knowing something in class already brought penalties and
the constant fear of punishment blocked the capacity to learn. The humiliation
and lack of confidence that accrued to bedwetters was just one more layer of
hurt in a cruel regime where care for even the most basic elements of bodily
and psychological development was absent. Tired, sore and humiliated, children
were unable to learn.

But you had (pause) you could never learn anything. Never learn anything.
Because what used happen was that (pause) seventy lads there, seventy
kids there and forty or fifty of them used to wet the bed so the beating
would go on for about an hour every day. They would just start beating
the backside off you with a hurley stick and that would say (pause) go on

for an hour. So if you are in an atmosphere like that and you are trying to learn you know, you can't do it. I was a 'wet the bed'. *Derek*

Carol is now in third level education but remains insecure about written skills and still has trouble sleeping.

We were called I would say about half a dozen times during the night to go to the toilet and hence you know (pause) I would still wake up and this is no exaggeration between seventy-five and eighty times a night. I would love to know what it is like to sleep through the night. *Carol*

Material resources

The major root cause of all resource deprivations was economic inequality and contemporary literacy inequalities reflect how similar injustices persist today (National Economic and Social Forum, 2009; OECD, 2009; Tett *et al.*, 2012).

At the time, those who had experience of schooling outside of institutions reminded me that class inequalities had impacted on learning there too. Both Dara and Kevin felt challenged to learn literacy in mainstream schools because they were unequally resourced both economically and emotionally. Dara remembered being beaten in school because she was unable to bring money for charitable donations and this distress further impaired her learning.

Because I came from a broken home and I would be going to school sometimes hungry and the other kids would be coming in happy and would be wearing nice clothes and I would be wearing old clothes. I was just different. And then they would have money and I didn't so every morning I would be bet [beaten]. *Dara*

I remember learning in school but I felt different. I had no school bag or books. I would be sitting beside a girl and she would be doing her homework. They were dressed different. There was something different. *Kevin*

Bourdieu (1986: 54) and Baker *et al.* (2009) argue that economic resources are 'at the root of all other types of capital' including the cultural capital that comes from education. Not surprisingly then, a large number of the factors that enable literacy learning care were in the past, and continue to be determined by economic capacity: levels of family literacy; awareness of the value of education; access to reading materials and knowledge of how to use them for language and literacy development; physical and mental health; time and presence. Other factors such as desire and willingness to use one's resources for the facilitation of another's literacy are more directly located in the affective domain but still strongly constrained and determined by levels of freedom that come from relative economic comfort. Unmet literacy needs do not occur equally across society today and socio-economic factors continue to determine literacy outcomes. Similarly, during the childhood experience of the respondents in this study there were hierarchies of privilege. Survivors repeatedly identified those who were poorest as the individuals and groups whose educational needs went unmet.

> Well it is far from equal rights for everyone. I think that we all have to understand that we didn't all come from a high background. If my mother had had money she would have sent me to higher education but she had nothing. You can even see it nowadays. You can see it with Irish Travellers for example. They are the ones that don't get education today… and the poor people. It is still happening today.   *Susie*

Literacy learning resources

Many respondents cited little or no access to literacy resources, toys, games or other material stimulus to develop either spoken or written language. Tania remained incredulous that their lack of resources went unchallenged by those to whom it should have been evident.

> I just can't understand why they didn't ask why there are no books, or a library or that the children didn't possess anything. I don't think I had one possession during fourteen years of industrial school. Not even a pencil. It was handed out and handed back everyday. We had nothing.
>   *Tania*

In one school, only one children's television programme was shown each week and this privilege was frequently withdrawn to punish some transgression. One woman recalled that the library books in her classroom were only available twice a year when the state inspector was present and then many of those who were given momentary possession of them were unable to read them. She remarked that they were, in any case, uninspiring for young children and that 'they had no pictures'. Other popular reading materials like comics were frowned upon in more severe regimes but where comics could be accessed or when they were permitted, they seemed to have been part of a more liberal, and effective learning care policy. More often the reading material was unstimulating and had a religious bias.

> There wasn't stimulation you know? There weren't clocks, there weren't newspapers, there weren't books in general and those things would be prayer books or hymn books those kind of things and the emphasis on that … so there weren't many materials around for people to explore at their own pace. I think that was the main thing. They weren't encouraged at their own pace or to develop or stretch themselves in terms of literacy or developing knowledge. *Counsellor*

Playtime

Matt was one man that had positive early recollections of care. He recalled happy experiences of Saturday walks when those who had been sent some money from home were allowed to buy sweets.

> We used to go on walks on a Saturday or Sunday and we would be going along through the town in D—. If you had money the nuns would know and they would hold the money for you and she would come along and say Matt would you like money for sweets. They would let you run into the shop. It wasn't too bad. *Matt*

Again he described summer holidays where children were able to enjoy carefree days and sweets were equally distributed each evening.

> I didn't experience any cruelty in the class. The only cruelty was with like say a boy who wet the bed. I think that they were very fair myself because you know we used to go to T— for six weeks for like a holiday and we lived in wooden huts and canvas beds. And you would have night-lights because there was no electricity. We enjoyed ourselves. Everyday we went

down to the beach and even if it was raining we would go for a swim. If it was a nice day we would stay down there for longer. And every evening we would go for a walk along the beach and then back but before we would go for the walk the nun that would bring us for the walk—and there would have been a lot of boys—she would have a can of (pause) what was sweets and they were individually wrapped. She would throw them in the air and the way it worked everyone got a sweet. I think they were fair enough.　　　　　　　　　　　　　　　　　　　　*Matt*

Elsewhere, play was only a physical activity and never structured around educational or even social objectives. For boys, one limited exception was the area of Gaelic games where talented participants were given some degree of respect. The narrative of one such gifted athlete revealed that he and others from sporting teams were given assistance with their primary certificate exams as part of some sense that illiteracy should not besmirch the mantle of hurling or handball champion.

I was into sports, handball, Gaelic, hurling. We used to go out and play teams. We had a league outside so I had it handy that way. I could play the sports. I don't know what could have happened if I hadn't been playing sports. They wouldn't leave you marked on the legs because we were playing a match outside and they were cute that way. When I was doing the Primary Cert., I told the Brother I didn't know the answers so they told me them because they were embarrassed for me. There was some people they helped and others they didn't. They had high hopes for me you see.　　　　　　　　　　　　　　　　　　　　*Jim*

Aside from these particular favours, play was merely an unstructured moment of liberty in the schoolyard, overseen by unpredictable disciplinarians whose primary goal was control rather than the care, enrichment or development of their charges. For some, by an early age, play was already supplanted by work obligations.

I wasn't in the circle of play you know, doing anything like that, because I was working the whole time, doing chores around, polishing the shoes and all …　　　　　　　　　　　　　　　　　　　　*Laura*

I don't remember playing much but I remember we had jobs to do. *Pam*

Martin was in care from birth but because of a continued link with his mother he benefited in some small material and educational way from the economic and cultural capital of others.

I did have reading material because of my mother but I would have been possibly the only one. You see where she was working; she was a cook in a house, a domestic servant but it was a rich house and there were two sons. There were books around and if they didn't want the books or they were throwing them out she'd get them for me.   *Martin*

Martin's mother held him and his learning constantly in mind between her monthly visits. Such small affective and material advantages emerged as significant in accounts of why some learned literacy and others did not.

Human resources

As well as the affective presence of a parent or alternative primary carer, the resource issues of health, time and competence emerged in terms of both adult carers and survivors themselves. Frequently, parents who struggled in a context of massive resource inequality had neither the health nor stamina to look after their children's learning needs. Once in the care of the institutions children themselves often found that health factors detracted from their learning capacity. Physical and mental health issues associated with emotional and bodily deprivation and abuse, diluted survivors' capacity to participate fully in the meagre learning on offer. Some were not given any chance.

They would have been labelled almost from day one as being stupid. If you were six and you couldn't fulfil a job like shining floors you were no use so they would look for a way to get rid of you. They used to bring in someone to assess you and this person would assess you and you would be shifted into a mental institution. My sister ended up in such a place. She has been there all her life. She never had any schooling. And my sister could talk but she was terrified and she was coming on a bit at six but she wasn't coming on fast enough to do the tasks they wanted her to do and so she was discarded. So there wouldn't have been any sense that she should be allowed to learn to read and write.   *Brenda*

An alarming proportion of those interviewed reported hearing difficulties that were attributed to physical abuse or 'clatters' to the head. This was corroborated in the accounts of professionals and my own observations working and talking with a range of individuals.

> If you weren't doing what ever you were doing fast enough to satisfy the person you would get a slap. That was the system. They would get their hands and slap the two ears together. People say that is not what caused your hearing difficulties. But you know as well as I do how many people are walking around this centre with hearing difficulties. That couldn't possibly be coincidence. Not only that they used to say 'I will make your ears ring for a week' so they knew that they were hitting you with force. And they meant to hit you with force.   *Gill*

Few respondents could remember ever having benefited from time invested in the emotional or physical labour that forms part of learning care. Matt had been placed, until the age of ten in an institution about which no complaint had ever been made and had enjoyed a liberal, creative primary education where he felt noticed and cared about by the staff. This experience was not shared by any of the other respondents who were in different institutions.

> But I enjoyed it. There was a lot in the class. I can visualise even now where I sat in the class. I don't know what age I was—I could have been about eight—but she seemed to be a very good teacher. Now and then your concentration would wander and you wouldn't remember and then you would wake up. I remember her teaching me the time but it was very interesting. Yeah I used to enjoy it in the classroom.   *Matt*

Within the other institutions respondents had never individually, or in a group received a positive supportive approach to reading, writing, playing games or any aspect of language or literacy development. Those, whose home-life had involved some positive experience of literacy care, where the importance of education was made explicit, inevitably had more enthusiasm and confidence about learning.

> There are darker alleyways where I don't like going into but where the sun shines is where me dad was teaching me.   *Gary*

Reading and writing were taught as whole group activities—or as Jackson (1964) described *batch learning* and outside school time there was no opportunity for encouragement, support or practice of these skills.

Poverty and the need to spend time at work as a child kept Gary from school and eventually led him into care for a number of years. As an adult, his literacy was all learned since leaving school and he valued words highly as a writer and successful actor. Nevertheless, he had also rebuilt his life after years of addiction, homelessness and living on the streets and from his perspective, learning literacy was only part of the survival curriculum.

> You don't have time for learning so you don't have time to become a good student at anything but you do become a survivor and a good student of life.
>
> *Gary*

Like food, time devoted to another's needs was also used to symbolise love and care in many narratives. Liam had learned what little literacy he knew since leaving institutional care. He described a necessary partnership between parent and teacher in terms of the time available for learning. With his own children's literacy he was clear about how spending time was a vital resource in a loving and a learning relationship although he was less well resourced to help with literacy.

> I keep coming back to this. It is between the parent and the teacher. I am not with my child as much as the teacher is. When I look at her now and think back, I had nothing; but I spent as much time with her as I could. I used to read to her stories at night; teach her some words that I know and spend time with her. I gave her my time and my love and my daughter and my son know how much I care about them.
>
> *Liam*

Liam highlights the growing pressure placed on parents today to be their child's teacher although they may have been ill resourced for the position. This repeating pattern of under-resourcing has a cumulative impact on the literacy capabilities of generations within families and is increasingly the case as the pedagogical burden shifts from school to parent (Hegarty and Feeley, 2010; Smyth and Isserlis, 2003).

Competence

In the industrial school where most family influence had been removed, the only influential literacy care resource for residents was the classroom teacher. Unfortunately many of the teachers within the schools were unqualified and correspondingly unskilled (Raftery and O'Sullivan, 1999). Even pupils who were literate before moving into care regressed in the uncaring environment of the 'inside' school and classroom. Those pupils with any form of learning difficulty were given no specialised support and individual learning needs were ignored. Jennifer had competently learned literacy through an adult literacy scheme but is resentful of her neglect earlier in life. She attributes this both to time and a lack of awareness of how to facilitate her as a learner.

> I don't think they had time. It was a special school and they should have had some understanding and (pause) more time for you but they didn't. And it felt like a terrible empty thing really. Like you go to school to learn and you didn't get educated which was very annoying and embarrassing.
>
> *Jennifer*

Without the necessary teaching know-how, learners' needs went unmet yet the responsibility for this failure was frequently misplaced. Children were punished for wrong answers and failing to understand what was dictated rather than explained.

> Time is number one in helping someone to learn to read and I suppose time in a couple of different ways. You can't bully something into someone. You can't bully something into someone who is trying to learn how to read. The person can only go at his or her own pace and that is again individual. Because something worked with one student doesn't mean that it is necessarily going to work with another student. I think that you have to work out a different plan for different students. *Gill*

Ultimately, the State sanctioned the employment of untrained teachers and that in turn resulted in a lifetime of lost opportunity for the children taken into its care. The Kennedy report (1970) refers to industrial schools being 'inadequately staffed' and the Department of Education and Skills (2002) cites Kennedy as finding.

Most of those working in industrial schools and reformatories have no proper qualifications for their work … there appears to be a tendency to staff the schools, in part at least, with those who are no longer required in other work rather than those specially chosen for child care work.

Department of Education and Skills (2002:12)

There were concerns several times which are very well documented in relation to the skills of people who were teachers, unqualified teachers and the range of curriculum and the limitedness to catechism and first communion and confirmation and Irish history.   *Counsellor*

Martin who became a lifeguard and member of mountain rescue team on leaving care describes the blurring of responsibility for learning failure as unfair.

There's no such thing as pupil failure; it's teacher failure. In my view if the teacher has a classroom of willing pupils he should be able to teach the subject and be in command of it himself. It's the teacher; it's not the pupil who should feel responsible.   *Martin*

Many respondents were aware in some way, even as children, that resources and standards of competence were wanting.

I was in the 'inside' system but there was never a book given to you or hope that you would be able to perform or read out loud or anything like that. In actual fact the teachers weren't trained teachers so we were at a disadvantage straight away because they wouldn't have had Department guidelines as to what standard a child of my age would require. *Brenda*

In the industrial school, where scant resources were unequally distributed, it is interesting to look at those who managed to learn literacy.

Who learned and who did not?

Even within the regimented system of the industrial school, children were differently resourced in terms of the material and human resources that encouraged their learning efforts. The affective privation and deprivation that underlay all their childhood experiences was demonstrable in their poorly resourced learning care although documentary evidence has been found that shows many parents tried to resist the system and maintain contact with their children.

> And most of them didn't have any family looking out for them and I think that is the key thing too. I could see from some of the files that came through that some parents because they were out on the streets or hadn't paid rent that the kids were taken away from them into care and they wanted them back and they wrote these heart-rending letters to try and get them back. But their circumstances were so poor that they didn't. But they used to come and visit and I think that that is what kept some of those kids just with a toehold in normal life or in care. That was a vital thing I would have said that there was somebody looking out for them and there was someone belonging to them.   *Psychologist*

In the schools, there was little care or joy in the process of learning to decipher and encode the printed word and although some miraculously developed a love of literacy this was frequently attributable to a more compassionate past when learning care was more generously resourced.

> My life has been a pattern of in and out of care but I have very vivid memories of my life before I went, say when I was three or four… learning words at home with my mother… storytelling. And then when I did go to school we weren't allowed to eat until our homework was done. There is a bit of a perfectionist in me as well and maybe it's because I remember my mother always checking over our homework. You need that kind of approval. It is a kind of a nurturing thing you know?   *Carol*

Where families had the literacy resources themselves they were better placed to pass these on to children. This suggests that expectations of parents today should take account of parent's own opportunities for literacy skills development. Where major inequalities of condition continue to exist today and resources are not made available to redress them then unequal learning outcomes are likely to persist through successive generations.

Those who had even a small taste of positively resourced literacy experience prior to institutionalisation can attribute some lasting learning benefit to that.

And I remember her going through the alphabet with me and things like that. I had a lot of books as a child. My grandfather and grandmother would have been good readers. My father would have been a good reader as well and when we were small we were brought to the library and that. I would have had comics too. She was great my Mam! She was a great woman.   *Una*

I do think that when I look back that it must have been because like I had a good life before I went into care. When I was at home I wanted to learn to read and write. Like I would take the books out and look at them and want to read them and try and write my name on them. I know that I mustn't have been able to but I know that I wanted to and I know that I tried to read even then. Even though I am not a great reader I would still read books. I would read anything.   *Dara*

The practical care resources deployed by those who could visit their family members, write letters or make a financial or material contribution to their child's life often made a difference to their literacy outcomes. The pivotal difference made by material resources was obvious even to the children who were utterly dependent on the state.

I was aware that they were going home and that they were better dressed than we were and the lunch they had and what we got was completely different. The books they had half the times we didn't have. The cookery classes we spent the whole time standing around with our face to the wall because we didn't have the ingredients to do the cooking. So I knew that something was amiss—that I was different from them.   *Tania*

Those who received comics or books from visiting parents, or who were taken in by a foster family for weekends, benefited from any literacy activity in that home. Sometimes this advantage was shared in solidarity with others.

I used to bring back comics from the [foster parents] and we'd all collect in the middle toilet because they just couldn't tolerate us reading. I'd be reading out as most of the others couldn't read and they would be looking at the pictures. There were six in at a time and a queue was outside the door. We were in a fantasy world for those few minutes with that comic!

Clare

Martin had experience of two different industrial schools. The first had a more benign approach to reading in that it allowed books and comics and most of the boys there were literate. When it closed, he and his peers were moved to a harsher regime and he was aware that his literacy levels were well in advance of others in his new peer group. He attributed this to the learning offered in the first school but more importantly to the additional resources and encouragement his mother provided for him. It was clear from his statements that he was confident in his own ability and took comfort from the escape that reading provided.

> I remember being in [name of school] where my mother gave me copy books belonging to the son of the house where she worked or something that I was able to copy and get to know it better just as I got to know from the books. I got to know stuff that we didn't really do. If I hadn't had that I certainly wouldn't be, I certainly wouldn't say illiterate but it certainly would have taken me longer to learn.
>
> *Martin*

For a short time, when she was a teenager Laura remembered someone spending some compassionate time with her that gave her some rudimentary literacy skills and a sense that she did in fact have the ability to learn. In later life she was able to build on the thin sliver of self-belief that this encouragement seeded and to improve on these small beginnings.

> And she would sit with me and spend time with me and I knew then that if I was given the time and the understanding I could have been capable of learning.
>
> *Laura*

Where no encouragement was provided and children's work commitments stole time from studies it was personal resources and survival skills that kept a small number of children succeeding against all expectations. Professionals working with survivors confirmed that conditions and attitudes within industrial schools were not conducive to learning literacy. Material and relational factors were important, as were issues of time spent in care and away from family. It is a tribute to children's natural resources and capacity for resistance and survival that any learning occurred within such a loveless environment.

State duty to resource equality of learning care

That the state failed in all aspects of its duty to resource the care and education of children in industrial schools is not disputed. The empirical data provided by this study confirms this and adds detail to the specific and still neglected field of literacy learning in institutions. The basic, material and human resources needed to provide a caring learning environment were all flawed and more often than not negatively influenced survivors' capacity to learn literacy. State checking mechanisms failed to ensure that either the basic physiological or the affective resources were provided and this left a legacy of unmet literacy needs both to individuals, their families and the state itself. Where narratives inevitably connect with current literacy learning, evidence of persistent resource inequalities emerges that is familiar to survivors.

> In my day the people who had literacy difficulties were the people who came from big families. Yeah, poor people didn't get a chance. It is still going on today. These schools in disadvantaged areas—the teachers never get no relief. They are just trying to get through the day. They know that these fellows won't get on. They don't put more effort into them. They just say, "Oh thank god it is three o'clock". If a kid comes from a disadvantaged family then the teacher just thinks that they are wasting their time. *Kevin*

Kevin described how the affective quality of his children's learning had been impacted upon by contemporary wider inequalities of condition and the unequal expectations that may accompany them. Literacy discourses today reflect this persistent impact of structural inequalities on literacy outcomes and the manner in which literacy acts as a barometer for wider social inequities. (National Economic and Social Forum, 2009; OECD, 2009)

Bob clearly names the state duty for literacy learning care provision. As someone whose special needs in terms of dyslexia were never catered for he is passionately insistent on the state's responsibility to resource individual learning needs.

> It is the state that is responsible. It is the school. The children are in primary school and the teachers see young children who can't read and

write and talk to the parents and things are put in place for these children to learn. That is how the system works. And if that is not done the state is responsible for these kids not being able to read and write because at the end of the day, taxpayers are paying money to make sure these children are educated. And if there are young children who can't, and they find it difficult learning literacy skill, something has to be put in place for these kids to learn.   *Bob*

Resourcing literacy for adults

The Lighthouse Centre was established, by survivors, to provide education as healing to those who had survived the care-less learning environments of the industrial school. In an holistic ethos of care the Centre provided supportive, well-resourced opportunities for adults to learn in an unpressured environment. Tutors were sensitive and attentive to learners' specific learning and care needs. The content and process of literacy learning was consciously designed to be the antithesis of learning in the past. The contrast was constantly remarked upon by survivors as their combing and sorting of the past continued. In social areas of the centre, while reading the paper and drinking tea, pedagogical values and practice were mulled over and conclusions drawn.

Conclusions

It was clear in the empirical evidence how resource inequalities played a fundamental causal role in the literacy outcomes of survivors of abuse in industrial schools. They influenced the amount of vital affective support available to literacy learning and often were the defining factor in determining whether literacy needs were met or not. The empirical data describes the crucial role that human and material resources played in enabling the labour that made learning care a reality. Those who were denied even the basic resources of bodily nourishment, security and kindness did not have the energy, motivation or peace of mind needed to learn.

In the extreme environment of the industrial schools where many did not learn even the basics of literacy, those who had some parental contact or even the memory of it, those who had some reading materials or competent teaching, all benefited from that stimulus. They attributed their learning to even small advantages over their peers. Any time, interest and kindness given were significant and counterbalanced the otherwise impoverished learning environment.

Survivors who learned literacy as adults had to overcome the legacy of past learning patterns. They were articulate about the need for an individualised, sensitive approach to literacy teaching and learning. They also described the pressure on them as parents to support their children's learning when they have a dearth of experience to draw on for that work.

As well as making clear the need for resource equality in literacy care work, these findings highlight the extent to which families actually resource and support the learning of literacy. It follows that in allowing structural resource inequality to persist today, states perpetuate learning inequalities like those experienced by respondents. Evidence suggests this is not merely an historic matter and may explain why unmet literacy needs emerge today in schools that are situated in areas designated as disadvantaged. More and more frequently pressure falls on ill-resourced parents to accept culpability and to reduce the deficit caused by structural class and resource-related inequalities (Gregory and Williams, 2004).

When considered alongside respect, recognition and power in the chapters that follow, it is clear that resources are significant in establishing the quality of the affective experience for literacy learners, whether they are children or adults.

Chapter 5

Lessons about a culture of learning care: Literacy and the affective/respect and recognition interface

We were second-class citizens. We didn't exist in the classroom. We just were sitting in the back and we were never asked anything. Never! (Tania)

Cultural aspects of learning and in particular status-related inequalities impacted significantly on the experiences of learning care and literacy outcomes of the research participants. As with affective and resource inequalities, even small differences in degrees of respect and recognition impacted on literacy outcomes. Within the harsh circumstances in the industrial school a child's ethnicity, disability status, social class and other identity factors triggered additional inequalities within an already disadvantaged community. Time and time again, survivors attributed their harsh experiences of literacy learning to their disadvantaged place in the social order, their spoiled identity and the low or negative expectations that powerful adults had of them. Raftery and O'Sullivan (1999: 312) describe how those in industrial schools were assumed to be 'children of no value' who were being prepared to take their place as the docile servants of wealthy families or as domestic labourers for a range of religious establishments and enterprises. Social class was a defining discrimination, which in turn illustrated the pivotal influence of economic equality. The same religious orders that prided themselves on the quality of education provided to the privileged classes did not see fit to ensure that the children in industrial schools acquired even basic literacy skills. Ironically a proportion of these children were originally incarcerated for truancy.

Such socio-cultural links to literacy disparities are not confined to history but emerge in most recent studies of school-based literacy where those in Irish fee-paying schools are two years ahead of less advantaged peers (OECD, 2011). Across Europe and other places, literacy measures suggest that ethnicity, class and other devalued identity factors are still associated with literacy inequalities. There are constant evidential reminders that inequalities in the socially-situated literacy context remain as relevant today as in the dark days of industrial schools

(Commission of the European Communities, 2008; Eady *et al.*, 2010; OECD/ Statistics Canada, 2005).

The prevailing cultural climate

The pre-Celtic tiger Ireland of the 1950s to 1980s, when the research participants resided in state 'care', was highly influenced by traditional and religious values. The power of the Catholic Church in the then recently formed Irish State extended to all aspects of society. The church ran hospitals, schools, teacher training colleges, reformatory and industrial schools and a range of other institutions. In the case of the Christian Brothers there was a merciless zeal in relation to preserving the Irish language that made literacy in any tongue unlikely.

> Sometimes in institutions there was an emphasis on nationalism in terms of history and language. I know a good number of people who couldn't cope with the environment and couldn't cope with Irish on top of that and would be severely punished for what was perceived as truculence or avoidance of Irish. That would extend into play as well in regards to sports. There was punishment in the Christian Brothers' school for any boy who was seen playing soccer as that was seen as a betrayal of Irishness.   *Counsellor*

National morality was dictated by Roman Catholic doctrine that also defined the values underpinning the state legislative processes and the education system. At the same time, the state system of social welfare was embryonic and the church also controlled any charitable alternatives to state aid (Clancy *et al.*, 1995; Inglis, 1998). Those who became residents in Irish industrial schools were frequently victims of the wider opprobrium directed at adults who, in addition to being poor, had breached the moral and cultural code of the day. Within these institutions a particularly harsh version of the national cultural value system operated and the inequalities in wider society were intensified, reflected and reproduced. The lower levels of literacy outcomes in industrial schools than in wider society are a correlated manifestation of these disparities (Raftery and O'Sullivan, 1999).

Community collusion

Anger amongst ex-residents of institutions against the wider community reflected a view of collusion between the state, the church and civic society that allowed the disrespect and ill treatment of children to go unchallenged.

There was nobody in that town that stood up and if they had then this wouldn't have happened. It was one big clique. The nuns would come into the room and there would be respect. It was the power of the church and that is why there was nothing done and it went on so long.   *Gus*

Some of those interviewed were able to differentiate between adults who were kind and those who were not. They were also able to identify when they or other older children reproduced the culture of oppression and disrespect by behaving cruelly towards their peers. For the most part, any kindness was negated by the fact that there was no one who challenged the brutality and inequality and thereby changed the day-to-day reality into something bearable. Bridget described a cultural context devoid of social solidarity.

They [the state] created a very unfair system. Like I say it was all about the have-nots being slaves for the haves who would be like doling out a bit of charity every now and again and that was perfectly acceptable. None of them lived according to their own so-called beliefs. This drives me mad—the arrogance of people. The 'my parents have money and therefore I am somebody' instead of thanking their lucky stars that they have such privilege and sharing it amongst those that don't or contributing in some way that is meaningful for everyone. And filling the coffers of the church on Sunday when their neighbours next door were starving. It is the cruellest thing in the world for the adults of the country to do to the children of the country. And how can you expect people to respect citizenship in any form if there is no way for them to understand it and if there is no way of communicating it to them?   *Bridget*

Survivors recounted how they experienced the disrespect of the wider community. The children from industrial schools had abuse shouted at them in the streets when they were taken out for walks. They learned that it was somehow acceptable that those in nearby communities mocked and pilloried them. When they were 'boarded out' in families they were not allowed to eat with other family members. One woman related how the husband in a remote border farm, where she was sent to work aged thirteen, sexually abused her. She was returned to the school by the man's wife and told by the nuns that she was responsible for the incident. She had no knowledge or language to even explain what had happened at the time.

In general terms, those who internalised this sense of worthlessness lacked the self-respect that enables learning. If a child had no other affective point of reference then this deprecating influence was unmitigated.

The culture of care in industrial schools

The culture of care varied from institution to institution. Respondents report that they were often supervised by those who had spent their own lives in institutions and were consequently unfamiliar with the basic rudiments of affection and respect. Others who moved from one establishment to another were able to remark on qualitative differences in the way they were treated.

> We used to think [the first school] was awful but I tell you when we went to [the second school] we felt it was like a concentration camp and [the first school] was like a garden party.   *Martin*

From the relative kindness of his early childhood care Matt moved to a harsher regime for boys aged ten and over. He observed a gendered difference in terms of both the aesthetic and affective environment.

> These men were in black whereas the nuns were soft like with their blue habits. And when you went in there were all these big people and there was no colour anywhere. Like even in the convent there was colour everywhere.   *Matt*

Not everyone experienced the softness of the nuns. Many reported physical, emotional and psychological abuse at their hands. Others observed a strong sense of contempt and disrespect directed towards them that was related to perceptions of their family of origin.

> I think that we were made to pay for any sins—for our parents. We were made to pay for that. I reckon that they didn't like us. We had to repent for what our parents had done. We were sinners.   *Tania*

Others saw their treatment as part of a mission to control the morality of the nation. This was clearly done in a manner that was both patriarchal and misogynist and explains why some children were allowed contact with family members while others were not.

One particular girl has told me that her father had run off with another woman and so her mother was left alone but she found another man and that was deemed not proper. So the next time the woman came up she was told "Oh you don't come. You are a bad example to your children and we don't want that". They were judging people's morals and they had no right to do that. They weren't in charge of the mother they were in charge of the child and so it was up to them to teach the child proper morals not to judge the children on their mother's morals.   *Jane*

Unequal expectations

Although the proclamation of the new Irish State had proudly aspired to 'cherish all the children of the nation equally' (McVeigh, 1995), in practice, the educational expectations of those in industrial schools were particularly unambitious. Respondents were aware that they were being groomed to join an army of 'skivvies and cleaners' that would be deployed at minimal cost across church-controlled establishments. For this reason those in teaching roles had limited interest in ensuring that literacy was equally distributed. Obedience and drudgery were the only required characteristics for those whose place was determined at the bottom of complex hierarchies of respect and recognition.

There was scant recognition in residential care institutions for the developmental aspect of childhood. Accordingly, work, usually an adult affair, was a major feature of life in the industrial schools. The religious orders ran many enterprises both as a form of vocational training and supplementing their *per capita* education grants from the state. Even very small children were part of the schools' labour force.

> The truth is that we were slaves. It was a slave economy. I have no doubt about it.   *Bridget*

> There was never anybody else hired to do the cleaning in that cold convent. It was always us girls. No contract cleaners and no employed women. It was us. And we had to clean that place every morning and every evening.   *Mona*

One woman told me that at the age of twelve she was responsible for over fifty young boys. Each morning she had to ensure they were washed, dressed, fed and ready for school before she had time to care for her own needs. A relentless work culture meant that children were often exhausted when they arrived in the classroom. In many cases they did not go to school at all.

> There was no literacy at all, absolutely none whatsoever. You were doing menial tasks when you should have been a child, enjoying children's things. You weren't exploring your mind creatively and you weren't utilising your mind in any real sense.
> *Gary*

As well as household tasks of cooking, laundry and cleaning, children stitched footballs, sewed socks, stuffed mattresses and made rosary beads. These were commercial contracts undertaken by the religious orders using child labour. Girls in one institution had targets for making sixty decades of rosary beads each night before going to bed. These were then taken to a factory and assembled into a saleable item. Some schools prided themselves on running self-sufficient farms and other enterprises using child labour. Such activities took precedence over learning and often interfered with continuity of schooling.

In a few cases work provided a welcome if unhealthy escape for children who were unhappy in school or with their peers. A psychologist suggested that this could create a submissive and isolated child who was dependent on an exploitative regime and without the hope or skills of becoming an autonomous adult. Laura was grateful, through work, to escape the gibes of teachers and peers about her lisp. She had to wait until she was sixteen before she realized that she was, in fact, able to learn literacy. As a child, small kindnesses gleaned while working, were still a better option for her than the cruelty of the classroom.

> They were very good. If I said something wrong, they knew what I meant and they didn't criticise. There was some people very kind and they would thank you for what you did. They can't say everything was totally wrong. I did (pause) learn to get a good pair of hands, and understanding of people. I did do sacristy, I did do (pause) I was allowed to bring people in and put them into their parlours and welcome them and none of them criticised me. And I was able to communicate. I think I was fairly good communicating that way but I was on my own then and I didn't have someone laughing at me. I was always very, very determined to prove myself.
> *Laura*

I can still see the sense of relief on the face of the kids who didn't have much literacy, because they were struggling, so when they were sent to do these menial jobs they were happy, I imagine. They could do the jobs and they were comfortable.   *Carol*

Ironically, in most cases, the working culture of the school was counterproductive in preparing institutionalised children for later working life. Their lack of literacy skills limited their chances and imposed restrictions on the support they could offer to their own children. It was short sighted and uncaring to limit children's development in this way and as adults, respondents described their despondency about their loss of opportunity.

And then if you don't have education people think that you are stupid, you are ignorant you are (pause) there is nothing to you. You are like nothing if you don't have education. It is so important. You can't rise above anything unless you have education. It is the key to everything. *Bob*

Others who, as children, had attended outside school were aware that literacy was important and described it as a 'ticket to freedom' or 'light at the end of the tunnel'. It became both a tool of survival and an investment in the future. Those who were sustained in an affective family framework were encouraged and motivated by that relationship or even the memory of it.

I remember that and I knew it was important in some way to be able to do that [learn literacy] in their eyes. I would have wanted them to be proud of me and I would have wanted them to know. And in actual fact I wanted to read for him more than for me because I wanted him [her father] to be proud of me.   *Brenda*

Evidence repeatedly suggested that expectations of children in institutions were low and resulted in masked ability and self-belief destroyed. Later in life, their retrieved school records, have sometimes painted a different picture to the one declaimed at the time. Tania was repeatedly told that she was worthless and unwanted and her 'stupidity' was directly associated with the absence of care in her life.

Oh stupid, so stupid you know. Completely brain dead. You will never amount to anything. All you will be good for when you go out of here will be domestic work, laundries and that kind of thing. But sure how could you be any other way? Nobody wanted you. How could you have any brains because nobody wants you? So how can you be clever? I must have been, because when I got my reports back it has the list on reading and writing and it says that I was very intelligent and I was only a young child then.

Tania

Learning culture—pedagogical practices

The approach to literacy in the industrial school, like that in the mainstream system of the day, was almost entirely mechanistic. Learning was a process of repetition and reproduction that excluded cognitive elements such as perception, understanding, intuition or reasoning. The methods used to facilitate reading, writing and spelling all relied heavily on auditory memory. Visual and kinaesthetic aspects of memory were less engaged other than in repetitive tasks. Many adults today continue a convoluted process of reading with their ears rather than their eyes in that they have to spell a word aloud before recognising and naming it. This proves to be a difficult pattern to break and is much more strenuous for learners than simple visual word recognition.

When we used to do reading we used to do it like a poem where you learn it off. And we used to be able to read like robots. And because my memory is good I would have been able to keep up and they wouldn't have known. I wouldn't have recognised the words and to spell them would have been beyond my ability. I had to repeat something over and over and this is with writing as well and this is how you learnt to do letters—not that you would know which word or context they would go into.

Jane

A number of those interviewed spoke of the impossible standards that were expected of children who were only at the beginning of a learning process. Mistakes were not tolerated and so children were trying to learn in a state of constant fear and tension. The demands of instant perfection meant that children were defeated before they began.

And perfection was another thing that they expected. What four-year old has a perfect stroke? That was expected of all children whether it was their ability. So from a very young age it was very rigid and you were afraid to go outside the lines. You know?   *Jane*

You weren't allowed to make a mistake in your copy. And dare you make a mistake and you would be murdered.   *Brenda*

Cultural alienation

In an environment characterised by oppression and the demonisation of difference, the manner in which literacy was taught, remained another means of domestication that quashed motivation. It excluded children from both the practice and the purpose of reading.

Books were only made available to children on rare occasions and then they were reportedly uninspiring.

Oh no. There was no joy (pause), never any joy in reading. If you were in a reading class you had to be silent. There would have been some books in a glass shelf and that was the library. And maybe twice a year (pause), one of those particular days was the day when some of the children would be there doing their Primary Cert. Now that was one of the days when you were allowed to take the books out if the Inspector was there and you would read them then. And then there was a day towards the end of the year too. But them were the only two days when you would get a library book out and have a look at them. And they were library books that were not suitable for children. Most children like to read about fairies and such like and these were about Irish history and other things we knew nothing about. They were very serious grown-up books. And what child wants to read that you know? Like and I mean. And you want to read a book if there are pictures. But that was never encouraged. You were totally discouraged from reading the Beano and the Dandy and all those kinds of things. They never wanted you to get passed a certain literacy level you know? To understand words that wouldn't make sense of your life.   *Jane*

In other instances, the reading materials of the day, if they were available, would have been alienating in that they presented images of a reality that had no cultural relevance for children who had either never known family life or been traumatically separated from it. As such, literacy materials and practice merely became part of a bigger lack of recognition and respect for children's circumstances.

> And then with a lot of the books—how do you make sense of the content of the books? It just doesn't fit in the same way as it would have done for others who would have gone to school, gone home and read about Ted and Mary and their pet dog and Daddy going to work in the morning. This stuff was foreign. There wasn't the actual (pause) there was no appropriate content even in the readers that they did have for people with such abnormal experiences. You are reading about something alien.
>
> *Psychologist*

Specific targets of disrespect

Within the wider culture of harm and disregard there were still further distinctions of rank and value. Those without any parental support and those who deviated from narrowly drawn norms attracted extra ill-treatment that in turn interfered with learning. Children were aware that some were more favoured than others and that this determined how they were treated particularly in the classroom.

> Probably the people who did learn [to read and write] were the brothers' favourites.
>
> *Paul*

> Like your mother was a prostitute. That would be thrown at you. They didn't give a damn. Yeah or if one parent had died you might have got slight sympathy. But for others whose parents like mine obviously didn't give a toss—well it was never going to matter whether we got an education or not. We really shouldn't have been born at all. We were 'born out of filth' and this is how we were seen. 'Oh, you black bitch. You little black bastard. Your mother ...'
>
> *Clare*

Orphans down the back

If literacy is a fundamental tool of rationality then the affective culture within which it is learned takes on added significance. Children in industrial schools were constantly made aware of how worthless the adults perceived them to be. Orphans were particularly vulnerable to unequal treatment in the classroom.

> We just sat in the classroom one year to another. The orphans down the back. Once we started the new class it would always be the orphans down the back. We weren't even allowed to sit with the day pupils. We were segregated.   *Tania*

People identified their position in the class as linked to perceptions of their ability and expectations of them as learners.

> If you are in a front row then you are closer to what learning is going on. If you are in the next one you are close enough but if you are in the far one you are not able to do it all. And in our situation I think that is what they done. Who they considered good at the front and then the next ones would have been semi-good but the poor unfortunates would have been left at the back—instead of getting all the children involved. *Jane*

> The way he had the tables set out it was like the best people in front and then people that were good and wanted to learn and then it was going back and back. There were different sections of the class. He knew exactly who was in the class and he put people who were slow or didn't show an interest at the back. I was at the back.   *Liam*

So access to learning care was signalled symbolically by position in the classroom. The act of being sent to the 'back of the class', both literally and metaphorically signified exclusion from the locus and potential for learning.

Diversity was not tolerated in the culture that demanded military-style uniformity in appearance and behaviour and extended this regime to the classroom. Those who were born outside of marriage, of mixed race or came from a nomadic Irish Traveller culture were pilloried and derided and culturally marginalised within their peer group. Gus and Clare were of mixed race and were frequently verbally abused and diminished because of their ethnic identity. Derek came from an Irish Traveller background and felt sure that inequalities of respect and recognition contributed to his unequal treatment and loss of opportunity in school. Social status issues subsequently disadvantaged him again when they were echoed in his treatment at the Redress Board. In his hearing it was suggested that his loss of opportunity, as a result of time spent in industrial schools, might be viewed as minimal because the general educational aspirations of an Irish Traveller would have been limited.

> Because I came from the Travelling background they were saying well (pause) 'You didn't lose that much opportunity'. But (pause) I had. Because I was taken into the institutions I should have had a better opportunity. You know? I should have learnt a hell of a lot more and I should have been someplace.   *Derek*

Left-handers

One day over coffee in the Lighthouse Centre, a man who was left-handed displayed scars on his hand where he was savagely beaten with a broken chair leg so that he would conform and become right-handed. Paul was comfortable using a computer but still moved into old emotional landscapes when he tried to write with a pen.

> I'm not a good writer with a pen. I suppose it's still that same fear again that comes to you or it's the thought of that that comes to you.   *Paul*

Like so many literacy patterns learned in the industrial school system, the fear of handwriting endures for Paul to the present day. Bridget too remembered punishment and verbal taunts related to left-handedness.

> I was a twin and we were both left-handed. We were beaten into writing with our right hands and I think it really upset our brains. I picked it up quickly but my brother didn't and he went through hell for it. They used to say it was evil—a sign of the devil and all that. 'I will beat the devil out of you.' I used to be frustrated that my brother didn't grasp it quickly enough to save himself from beatings.   *Bridget*

Individual needs

Those with particular learning care needs, those with learning difficulties or disabilities and those whose learning pace or style differed from the perceived norm were educationally sidelined. Bob's dyslexia went unheeded and he felt that no-one made an effort to develop his potential.

> To question what they were doing ... At the end of the day the sad thing is they were looking after someone else's kids. They weren't their kids biologically. And that was the sad thing. And I remember sitting through days and days of doing nothing [in school]. And in the children's home nobody ever asked anything. I can't remember anyone ever asking anything. But the whole set up wasn't geared (pause) the whole set-up was like a factory. You know? There were children there and if they had learning problems or emotional problems there was nobody there to deal with it.
>
> *Bob*

Others were publicly disparaged and no effort was made to discover appropriate ways to meet their diverse literacy needs.

> As a child I had a very bad lisp and I couldn't speak properly so when I was at school and trying to learn to read and write, if I got up to speak I was put sitting down again. I felt like a freak. I also felt (long pause) they always called me stupid and a dunce and when something is ingrained, embedded into your head, you take it that you can do nothing. I always say what held me back was reading and writing. You know, I always felt handicapped and nobody knows, will ever know from the inner depth of my body, how hard that was to take that you couldn't read or write and what good were you to society?
>
> *Laura*

Like many others labelled 'handicapped' at a very early age, Laura was taken out of school and put to work in the convent as a cleaner, a kitchen maid, and farm hand. She was sixteen before anyone took the time to introduce her to the basics of literacy. At fifty-nine she read and wrote quite fluently, was computer literate and involved in the support of her grandchildren's literacy development. She thought that schools still neglected individual learning styles and struggled so that her family would be given the understanding and care-full learning support that she was denied.

A limited understanding of learning and intelligences underpinned the industrial school ethos. Verbal and mathematical dexterity was paramount as indeed was the case in most schools in the country until relatively recently. In some institutions, ability in music or sport also attracted kudos for reasons more to do with nationalism and religious domination than individual abilities. Care for or about a child's talents and capabilities were not a feature of the learning culture. Children were told they were stupid in an extraordinary number of ways in both Irish and English. One of the few Irish words that many survivors know is *amadán*, which means 'fool'. They were called names and humiliated when they failed to repeat a word or a spelling. They were systematically and simultaneously undermined as human beings and as learners.

> They used to put a dunce's hat on me and they used to put me out against the wall and the teacher used to say, 'D is for Dara and D is for Dunce'.
>
> *Dara*

Several people spoke with regret of a colourless world where childhood exuberance was quashed and replaced with silence and strict control. One exception in this regard was Matt who lovingly describes his memories of learning to draw while others learned music nearby. He was unique in having had an opportunity to explore his creative preferences until at the age of ten he was moved to a more severe environment for older boys.

> One thing I used to like was that they used to give us a small book with tracing paper in it. It would be like sugar paper. Do you know what I mean? It was a book made up of that. And we used to draw in these books. We were taught to draw which was good. I remember drawing a bike; I remember that as clear as anything. Downstairs they used to do the singing. They used to teach the singing downstairs. Even though I loved the music I wasn't that interested in the singing. I think that I got a good grasp of learning when I was in the convent. I think I knew how to read and write when I left the convent.
>
> *Matt*

Consequences of disrespect—a loss of self

When they arrived at the industrial school, children were stripped of any trappings of individuality. Personal belongings and clothes were taken, uniforms issued and numbers allocated as a new mark of identity. This number, rather than a name was used to identify and address children in many industrial schools up until the 1970s.

> ... and we weren't called by our name; we were called by a number. Everything was marked in numbers. And (pause) I didn't know what age I was. Never had a birthday. *Laura*

The National Counselling Service established to address the emotional needs of survivors, highlights the importance of identity in the development process.

> Perhaps the most difficult of all to deal with is the damage that can be done to a person's sense of self and identity that can affect every aspect of their life and inhibit their potential for growth.
> (Health Board Executive, 2002)

Other professionals supported this centrality of identity to the growth of self-esteem that in turn creates the confident learner, able to grapple with the important early stages of literacy.

> I think that it is that you have to be able to set yourself in a story. It is vital. Vital. Because I mean if you are trying to learn stuff without knowing who you are and where you are going with that knowledge, it is like throwing salt at the wind because you have to have some kind of an internal consistency of '*us*' as an identity going somewhere. If you are just floating along at the mercy of other people you are not able to plan for tomorrow, let al.one next week. *Psychologist*

The consistency of 'us'

With the help of Barnardos and others, survivors spend considerable time trying to locate details of their schooling and family of origin. Sometimes this clarifies gaps in a personal history and reunites siblings after decades of separation. Often the search can produce little or nothing from inadequately maintained or non-existent records. One sixty year-old woman with whom I did one-to-one literacy confided that her sole wish was to have a small photograph of her mother. She wanted to see a family resemblance between herself and another human being and without that she continued to feel rootless.

The Compensatory Advisory Committee (Department of Education and Skills, 2002: 30) affirmed that some children in residential institutions were 'publicly belittled and ridiculed by being called, for example, 'stupid dunces' or 'smelly wet-the-beds', and that as a result they were stigmatised within the industrial school. Furthermore the committee heard allegations of racially motivated abuse that seriously damaged self-esteem and meant that 'even the brightest pupils' were relegated to 'low status occupations'. Many respondents reported how family vulnerabilities formed the basis of verbal abuse that staff employed to denigrate them. Such factors were used to taunt children in class and inevitably contributed negatively to learning.

> There was a lot of name-calling used against my family like and in someway we believed it. Because my mother had a breakdown and so when certain names were thrown at you, you began to believe it and in actual fact it was the case that they often called us 'cracked'. My mum's illness was used to belittle me and belittle my sisters and that was huge in terms of my literacy difficulties. As soon as I would stand up to read I would hear it ringing in my ear and I would expect myself to fail and so in actual fact it stopped me making the effort.   *Brenda*

Some just assumed that they were 'bad' and unlikely to succeed in any learning by virtue of the fact that they had been placed in an industrial school. Others were defamed more directly. Name-calling by adult 'care-givers' was a common form of disrespect and disparagement that belittled children and made absorbing literacy problematic.

Adult consequences of wasted potential and lost opportunity

Lack of learning care had not just left survivors' literacy needs unmet but also ensured that many were ill-prepared to participate fully in adult life. In extreme cases this had meant exclusion, marginalisation and even untimely death. A number from the community died prematurely during this study from addiction, stress-related physical and mental illness or taking their own life. Others damaged by abuse lived lives that took them to the street in prostitution and homelessness and into prison.

> A lot of the people that I know that can't read and write are homeless. They are out on the street with nowhere to go and (pause) very few of them can read or write. Those that were in institutions that never learnt. Lots of them people can't read and write.   *Vincent*

Gus thought that it was inevitable that he and others ended up in prison given how little care went into their learning and preparation for life. He was motivated to disprove the expectations of his early teachers and attributed his loss of opportunity to lack of stimulation and multi-faceted neglect in childhood.

> I believe that if I was brought up properly and decently and well fed and not being called this that and the other I would have made an effort. And it has taken me over forty years to do it and now I am doing it to show them. If I had been brought up properly I wouldn't be sitting here today. I would have made an effort but it was just that I was so low down and mistreated and not fed and the interest is gone. There was nothing there. You could have been sitting in the class but there was nothing there. I don't remember the teachers ever asking me.   *Gus*

Bob also spoke of being disregarded in a learning process that failed to engage with him and his needs. This misrecognition was an important feature of his experience and he felt he was left to 'stagnate' without anyone him into consideration. Consequently he was conscious of manifold cultural disadvantages and an absence of hope.

> There is a whole world that I have missed out on: libraries, sitting down with books, education. I've missed out on knowledge. I've missed out on a career. I've missed out on jobs. I've missed out on any dream that I could possibly have. The self-confidence (pause) because I don't have the confidence and I don't have the literacy skill. There is always this thing when there is something that I want to do. There is always this doubt in my mind that I can do it.   *Bob*

The Compensation Advisory Committee of the Redress Board saw lost educational opportunity in the context of industrial schools as 'serious neglect' (Department of Education and Skills, 2002: 29). Legal professionals working in the area of Redress believed that such attitudinal patterns that discriminated against children in industrial schools were being replicated in the Redress system that was supposed to bring them justice.

> There is no comprehension for loss of literacy in the court. I think that they have the view that if people are from a particular socio-economic background that nobody reads that much any way. That is just my view. They certainly think that people have to come from a particular social background to be able to read and to be able to appreciate any form of a book. If you can read the front page of *The Star* and the sports page then you are fine.   *Legal professional*

Literacy is such an integral part of all aspects of life that its absence can interfere with the essence of adult identity. As the demands of bureaucracy and the textual culture of the information society grow, those without literacy can become excluded and dejected. One woman I spoke to had given up on a business she had run for years when levels of bureaucracy increased and she could no longer cope. Others aspired to have a literate identity; to be admired for literacy proficiency and to be able to act autonomously in a world that expects adults to be literate even in their expression of affection.

> I would love to be able to write or for people to say, 'Oh you are a lovely writer'. If I get postcards sometimes from people I notice that they are a lovely writer. Somebody's birthday or anniversary I will get somebody who is a good writer in the family and I will get them to write the card. It is very difficult when someone says to you, 'Can you write this letter?' and then you can't.   *Kevin*

As part of the Redress process, survivors were given copies of their childhood records from the courts and industrial schools. For many this began a jigsaw puzzle of identity reconstruction. People wanted to peruse their retrieved personal records at a leisurely pace and to revisit certain aspects on more than one occasion. Even this was difficult if one was dependent on others to read these records aloud and the associated loss of privacy, dignity and independence was crushing. The arduous piecing together of memories and evidence to create a fuller picture of the past had become both therapeutic and compulsive as people tried to establish a coherent identity and make sense of the past. Many survivors had devoted time, effort and literacy skills to reconstructing their personal history.

I've written my own biography. And I've written that over a number of
years and there were a certain number of things that I had to rewrite and
rewrite and rewrite and it took me about five or six years.   *Derek*

Ex-residents of industrial schools often concealed their past because of the
stigma attached to having been in state care. They avoided naming the schools
they attended when completing forms and limited the information they divulged
about their childhood. As suggested by Goffman (1963) this concealment
impacted on adult relationships and often involved the wider family circle in
collusion to keep the past a secret.

Respondents reported that having unmet literacy needs exacerbated the
destructive emotions associated with their childhood. For Dara, having unmet
literacy needs felt even more shameful than having been in care.

Because I didn't know how to read and write when I left school, I suffered
all along. Like trying to hide it and trying to get by without certain things
when I didn't know what the words were. When I left school I could
hardly read at all. You can make excuses for care but for reading and
writing there are no excuses and that is the way that I feel. You feel that
you have no excuse and that you should be able to do it like anyone else
and then you try and hide it.   *Dara*

Not being able to perform in literacy events caused some adults to shun social
contact. Others talked about compensating by developing exceptional memory
skills and focusing on non-textual aspects of communication.

Recognition, respect and solidarity in adult learning

Although it is counter-intuitive for many adults with unmet literacy needs to
believe that they can regain their educational entitlement, this is the recurring,
hopeful story of adult literacy. Moreover the Lighthouse Centre had a particular
appeal in that it provided a culture of support and solidarity for those with a
shared experience of abuse. The politicisation of their oppression had created a
more respectful learning environment where stigma, silence and self-deprecation
was suspended at least when they were within their own community of interest.

I know that some of them had horrendous adult lives and their lives were
bettered immediately on coming to Lighthouse because they were with

people that they could identify with and more than that they were with people who could help them and were willing to help them and I think that was a huge boost to them. They could come out from this hidden hell that they had lived in; that had stopped them putting their head above the parapet and saying 'I am me'. Instead of hiding and holding their shame and pain and not being able to (pause) having no forum to express it in anyway except in law breaking or any other thing that came their way.   *Bridget*

I think that there is actually a lot of solace for people who maybe have felt quite alone that they come into a place and realise that people do have some form of shared history, some sort of shared continuing difficulties and that actually binds them together as a group. One of the features of the groups is that they do very much look out for each other, especially new members of the group. They try to welcome them in and a lot of support is actually peer-to-peer support.   *Lighthouse Centre worker*

The impact of the solidary learning environment was liberating for those who would feel intimidated about attending an adult class outside the community.

Well I suppose that one of the things that in social care we talk about when children are in orphanages or group living or cared for by people other than their parents, is that what they miss out is the special encouragement that parents give their child in terms of education; in terms of helping with homework; in terms of reading or in terms of trips to educational places and thinking of education in its wider sense; and the delight that a child takes if a parent is proud of them for the work that they have done. It wasn't just that survivors were in classes where the teachers weren't good but that the majority would say that teachers were actually cruel. And outside of all that, they were not receiving any of the positive attention that goes with having a family. I think that is maybe one of the massive deficits (pause) that this place fills. It fills that parental role of encouragement. And that's one of the things that the survivors rave about in here is that the teachers praise you. They don't expect to be encouraged by a teacher who they would see as an authority figure. But they also see them as slightly more than a teacher because of the closer relationship and the slightly smaller classes and so on.

Centre worker

This was not just to do with the tutors but with the motivating dynamic of the peer group.

I see people sitting in there and doing their own thing (pause) writing or talking or reading. And you know that is what this place is all about. It is about feeling comfortable and learning and growing and developing and feeling loved and everything like that. *Susie*

Those that succeeded in achieving personal change had also benefited from the care that encouraged a sense of self-respect and self-confidence. Beginning a new learning cycle in adulthood required that fragile self-belief to be consistently buttressed against self-doubt. The role of the centre worker, at the time, in supporting the move back into learning was respectful and firmly affective. It resonated with the qualities of the concerned primary carer that was absent in childhood.

A lot of people come back to me after the first couple of classes and they are beaming and they are delighted. And they are like 'I can't believe how good it is and the class is so nice.' And I get reports like that, which would lead me to believe that there is encouragement and solidarity. Even if somebody is struggling there is an understanding that it is not your fault. We are all in it together. And again that is why people would come here rather than going to another educational centre (pause) even with the same teachers, because the people in the class maybe have the same reasons for having problems. *Centre worker*

Literacy in an unequal world

The individual satisfaction that many adult learners got from being able to use literacy was not insignificant. Nevertheless Bridget articulated the need for literacy practitioners to remember that becoming literate in an unequal world can also open up a painful and unsatisfactory perspective from which there is no turning away. Time and again, adults were confronted with a reality in which they were culturally unequal and literacy alone would not redress the imbalance.

> And that is something that literacy people ought to be aware of, is how big a deal it is because it alters their lives completely. Personal responsibility comes into the realm of that because a person who gains the tools to view their world from a different perspective can never pretend that they don't have that perspective. You know? So it is a huge deal.   *Bridget*

Conclusions

Survivors articulated details of a culture in industrial schools that was reflective of wider society but that further intensified harsh and judgemental attitudes to those perceived to be of less social value. The poor and morally suspect were feared rather than nurtured and the task of the industrial school was to domesticate and control them to take their place at the bottom of the social order.

Those facilitating literacy learning in industrial schools did not create a culture of care in the classroom nor even ensure that all learners were equally included in the learning process. Children in these institutions were variously discriminated against as learners on the grounds of family status, class, race, ethnicity and other individual differences. Diversity was met with intolerance in a regime that sought to impose control and uniformity and the Catholic Church was a major force in legitimating this inequality. Individual identity and family influence was systematically effaced in efforts to create a docile and obedient underclass often without access to even the most basic educational currency. As well as wider status inequalities, learners' individual learning styles and paces were neglected to the extent that many left school with their literacy needs totally unmet. The learning culture was mechanistic and lacked creativity and recognition of how literacy develops. Most teachers seemed incompetent and disinterested in their learners or their well-being.

Those placed in industrial schools were not seen to be as valuable as other learners and so were not given equal educational access. Many were part of a child labour force that kept them from the classroom and left them ill-equipped for later life. Children were disrespected, denigrated and demoralised in terms of their learning ability. They did not always understand the long-term value of learning and their teachers' expectations of them were both low and unequal.

For many this meant that they were doubly stigmatised in adult life by having been in state care and by having unmet literacy needs.

Respondents in the research were able to identify hierarchies of respect within an already care-less environment and to make corresponding links to literacy outcomes. On the other hand, in the adult learning environment of the Lighthouse Centre, a culture of acceptance, encouragement and solidarity made a positive contribution to literacy outcomes and to rebuilding damaged learning identities. The Lighthouse, in the conscious creation of a healing, learning care culture, became the antithesis of the utterly care-less experience of life in the industrial school.

Chapter 6

Lessons about empowering learning care: Literacy and the affective/power interface

Despite the fact that orphanages were designed to educate us and protect us from the ills of society, we received only minimal education and most of us were illiterate. Lack of education deeply affected every aspect of our lives, leaving us unprepared for and fearful of the world outside the institution. (Bernadette Fahy, 1999:54)

Introduction

It is the ultimate irony that the state insisted upon monopolising power over the lives of individual children only to preside over their educational neglect. Previous findings chapters have illustrated the links between the care provided for children in industrial schools and their learning of literacy. In particular, the interface between learning care and resources and learning care and respect and recognition, have been explored in some detail in chapters four and five. Since all of these aspects of inequality are interconnected, the issue of power has already been implicitly evident in the discussion of care, resources and respect and recognition. Those whose families remained involved in their lives or who were fostered, benefited from other voices that could speak on their behalf and who might be perceived to represent their interests. Those with some resource advantage were less vulnerable, better able to resist against abuses and so lees constrained in their literacy development. Similarly, those with marginally more status received correspondingly less direct abuse and interference with their learning capability. Here the focus shifts specifically to the way in which power shaped the affective tenor of the institutions and of literacy provision made within them.

Freire argues that all learning inevitably involves the negotiation of power and in the critical case sample in this study, inequalities in pedagogical relations proved to be extreme and unpredictable (Freire, 1972). There was little or no evidence of democratisation of the educational process as advocated by Baker *et al.* (2004, 2009), but rather a totally authoritarian learning regime where the potential of children was arrested and damaged rather than developed. Neither at macro national level nor at the micro classroom level was power used in any positive way to support, enhance or encourage literacy learning for the most vulnerable and disadvantaged children in society. This is a chapter about childhood learning memories that are characterised by powerlessness and almost entirely devoid of any practice of learning care. Respondents' descriptions of power-related literacy learning are heavy with stories of humiliation, verbal abuse and violent corporal punishment. Rather than being given any voice in the learning process, both families and children were frequently silenced and denied access to information. Some children were given no opportunity to learn. Others were placed in such a fearful environment that they were too distressed to learn. A number of respondents had grasped literacy before being institutionalised and this was often attributed to a supportive, primary care relationship. Otherwise, whether literacy was learned or not was dependent on the survival skills and resources that an individual could muster to manage the fear that accompanied the extreme inequalities of power, in those strange places. The narratives constantly cite degrees of tension and angst as the dominant feature of their classroom learning, contextualised within a wider regime that controlled through enclosure, repression, abasement, terror and abuse of every conceivable kind.

In addition to the three levels of learning care relations explored in chapter three, the role of the state emerged as significant in enabling the individual's right to literacy, both then and now. The religious orders and lay teachers, the primary actors within institution classrooms, were the paid agents of the state with whom resided final responsibility for the care and education of these children. Ultimate power lay with the state to monitor, evaluate and adapt the quality of care and education within industrial schools and their record in this regard has been shown to be unsatisfactory (Raftery and O'Sullivan, 1999). Even today, in the administration of redress to those harmed within their schools, the empirical evidence in this book suggests that the state is still replicating old patterns of indifference, carelessness and neglect with regard to disadvantaged individuals and groups, in matters of literacy.

Systemic power

As is the pattern, the power-based learning care inequalities that were rife in Irish industrial schools had their roots in political structures that legitimated some voices and silenced others (Lynch and O'Neill, 1994). The acquisition of literacy today continues to reflect these patterns of power in wider society where those who are powerless are also less cared *about* and less cared *for* both at a systemic and micro level in education structures. The industrial school system was sustained by the collaborative efforts of both state and Church in Ireland. In most cases, for reasons of poverty and powerlessness, children were brought before the legal system, committed and passed into the hands of the Department of Education. It, in turn, funded the religious orders to run the schools that would be responsible for the children's learning needs and general welfare.

Even in current times, children are relatively powerless and in most jurisdictions, including Ireland, there is still a sense in which children are construed as property (Baker et al., 2009; Duncan, 1993). Fifty years ago and more, children had no voice in the legal proceedings that consigned them to institutional care and their family members were often powerless to act as advocates. Most cases before the courts were in some way related to economic inequalities and there is no doubt that power followed money. There is criticism that at a time of limited welfare provision, at no stage was it considered that public funding might be redistributed to improve the lot of disadvantaged families, rather than empowering religious orders and disrupting the family structure. This was despite both Church and state frequently proclaiming the importance of the family unit and family values and enshrining them in the Constitution of the State (1922: Article 41).

> That wasn't my fault that my mother died and my father couldn't look after us. The State would have been better off giving the money to my father or allowing a carer to come in, rather than paying for years in an institution.   *Tania*

Unlike most contributors who thought of the state as a separate and remote entity, Bridget defined a body inclusive of all citizens. In her narrative, she repeatedly spoke of collective and community responsibility for the events in industrial schools. In this she echoes a view stated elsewhere that the civic neglect of children in industrial schools was like the response of many German people to the Nazi persecution of the Jews. Raftery and O'Sullivan (1999: 318) speak of the 'peculiar phenomenon of people both knowing and not knowing at the same time, or perhaps more precisely, knowing enough not to probe any further.'

Bridget identified the root cause of unmet literacy needs and wider social dysfunction located in an individualistic ideological viewpoint and the absence of any real ethos of care for children or for the collective good.

Do you know it might sound simplistic but it is every adult's responsibility to ensure that every child is educated. If we all just look after our own— that is why we were the way we were. Those adults who couldn't look after us were equally abandoned by all the adults who could have helped out but instead abused them every way they could. At the end of the day, the question is who is looking after the children? Who is really caring about the children? That is always the question and it still is the question. People are leaving school today and they can read and write and debate and go out and smash a car and buy a car and they know all about interest rates and mortgage rates and they know nothing about feeling and caring. They are all *mé feiners*.[16] There is no sense of citizenship or loyalty to one another. It is all about me and me and me. Or mine. So there is some kind of huge discord around care for everybody, not just me and mine.

Bridget

Once consigned to the industrial school children were utterly powerless and the majority in the study had no one to speak for them or to defend their interests.

The ones like us didn't have any background. They would know where you came from. They knew you had nothing to stand on if you went complaining that the teachers were giving out to you because it would have been said back to them and then you would have gotten a wallop and there was just no use complaining really.   *Pam*

Without recourse to advocacy and often with little comprehension of their situation, children were reliant on the degree of justice with which regulations within the schools were administered. In reality, the regime itself was harsh enough but in addition to this, there were also abuses of that power.

Power enacted as regimentation

The regime in many industrial schools, particularly for older boys, was one of total authoritarianism where behaviour was conditioned by whistled commands. Martin described an environment that strongly resembled the process of creating 'docile bodies' outlined by Foucault in *Discipline and Punish* (1975). Enclosure,

---

16. *Mé féiner* is an Irish language phrase denoting those motivated by self-interest as opposed to those interested in the common good.

surveillance and the regulation of the body were part of a code of practice that aimed also to control and condition the mind and the whole spirit.

> We knew you see it just wasn't in the studying department. That's, if you like, a total human being thing; we were never allowed to be in charge of ourselves. Somebody else always dictated the curriculum not just the school curriculum but also the daily agenda so that was absolutely relentless. A whistle went for everything. You were marched everywhere. You were marched from the church up to breakfast. You were marched into class. You were marched to lunch. March here. March there. Fall into lines. All this and in all of these activities the whistle would go, which meant silence. You'd be into silence. Say the grace before meals. You'd sit down and silence for ten minutes. The whistle would go then you could talk and then ten minutes before the end, the whistle would go again and silence again. Up. Get out. March. Everything was robotic. Regimented.   *Martin*

The process of learning to write in a uniform manner epitomised a regimental form of literacy in line with the rest of the institutional ethos.

> I can remember little lines and little dots and you had to join the dots. They were little units; I mean what difference did it make if you went below the line? It was a ploy, a good excuse to give another beating to somebody.   *Jim*

Foucault (1975: 231) describes 'complete and austere institutions' as places of isolation, detention, routine and surveillance. Goffman (1961) had formerly described the 'total institution' as a place of extreme regulation, set apart from the rest of society and where a small number of staff wields power over a large number of 'inmates' or residents. Susie too described how the imbalance of power in institutional care obstructed the formation of a learning relationship. In fact it was wholly anti-relational. Enclosed, regimented and denigrated she withdrew from the literacy learning process for over fifty years, until the state apology to those in industrial schools permitted the opening of their adult learning centre at the turn of the century.

The teachers here are lovely but in the context of where we were learning we couldn't say that because we were treated like prisoners in a jail and if you are a prisoner in anything you just can't open up to people, can you? You can't open up to somebody who is going to traumatise you or make you feel bad. Can you?   *Susie*

Matt compared his two experiences of state care and highlighted the difference between his former school where there was relative freedom and the latter where discipline and the relentless assertion of power were dominant features of life.

Yeah, like the way you would be walking along the beach and you would have had freedom to roam around and there was no shouting like about keeping in line or any of that. You played and enjoyed yourself but when it came to the second place, everything was military from when you got up in the morning to late at night. It was all military formations and commands. And you would be punished if you went out of step. It was very strongly adhered to. Everything was military—even more military than the army. A commanding officer would be envious of the position and the strictness of the brothers and the boys.   *Matt*

Such regimentation, when it was enacted in the classroom, lead to a style of teaching reading that meant repetition rather than understanding. This practice of repeating words as they were pointed to on a blackboard, lead to children memorising a series of letters, rather than acquiring independent reading skills. In later life this meant that many just avoided reading as it has no pleasurable associations and they had never learned to read for meaning.

I missed out because I wasn't able to read it for myself and understand it. And it wasn't the reading; it was the understanding. And that can be very annoying.   *Jane*

Today, the legacy of that regimentation continues to make people hesitant about predicting a word or spelling in case it is wrong. They were discouraged from thinking autonomously or decisively and this has influenced every aspect of adult life.

> The other thing of course would be the whole issue of boundaries. That
> is a taught thing and that surprised me. If you have never had to make a
> decision in your whole life; if you have been living in an institution, your
> whole life and every decision has been made for you and how difficult it
> is then, at sixteen, to go out and actually start.   *Centre worker*

Martin maintained that the core purpose of the industrial school regime
was not one of care but one of subjugation of what was construed as a deviant
section of Irish society. This was done through the alliance of Church and state
who colluded to domesticate an underclass perceived as threatening both the
social and moral order.

> They wanted robots they could control with the least possible effort.
> They were good dutiful Christians who bowed when they were told. If
> you were to allow them any possibility of humanity they would have
> regarded it as they were trying to get as docile a population as they could
> without literally killing them. They were perfectly effective and accurate
> at it. That was exactly what they achieved.   *Martin*

Authoritarian control—an atmosphere of fear

This study produced more references to fear than any other generic theme.
Participants constantly described an atmosphere of terrible tension in the
institution as a whole, but especially the classroom where much time was spent.
They remembered being constantly watchful and alert to mood changes on
the part of the teacher and the ever-present threat of violence and humiliation
in front of peers. This hypersensitivity to atmospheres was apparent in the
Lighthouse Centre. If even small upsets occurred, people became quiet and
watchful until any tension was dispelled.

On arriving at the Centre first thing one morning we discovered that a break-
in had taken place during the night. A lot of mess had been made. One of the
intruders had cut himself and there was blood and excrement on a number of
surfaces. There was a palpable sense of violation. The police were alerted and
notices placed on doors to say that the Centre was closed for the day. Meanwhile
the small group of eight or so survivors who had arrived early made tea and
gathered in a tight group around a board game in which they became instantly
immersed. In all my years in the Centre, I had never seen them play such a game

before or ever again afterwards. It was as if they instinctively and collectively withdrew from the reality of the moment until the worst of the upset had blown over and then went quietly home.

In the course of the day in the institutions, Bill recalled boys fainting and getting sick as they waited for the teacher to come into the room. He dramatically conjured up the image of one Brother who, with the help of a long window pole, could hit a boy in any part of the room.

> But the fear in that place was (pause) the fear of not the unknown, but of knowing exactly what was going to happen to you.   *Bill*

For Brenda fear was a paralysing, almost solid presence that pervaded the whole institution.

> Fear was huge. When I first went to [the industrial school] and I went into the porch I didn't know what the feeling was. It was fear. It was only afterwards that I realised that what was hanging in the air was fear. I was coming from a homely situation and I couldn't understand this and for the first year I didn't know whether I was coming or going. I blanked out my first year.   *Brenda*

Bridget evoked the relentlessness of the terror. She felt worn down by the constant emotional pressure that was the very antithesis of learning care.

> Day and night there was just no respite from it. If we could have rested— had some rest, but we had no rest. There was constant (pause) I don't know how more of us didn't drop dead from the strain or from emotional pressure. It never ceased to amaze me how much the human spirit can take and we took a lot. They were torturing us. And expecting children to learn literacy or anything in that and I know the vast majority didn't.   *Bridget*

The ineffectiveness of a tyrannical approach to teaching literacy was clear to most respondents. The point is sometimes made that such corporal punishment and authoritarianism was the educational order of the day but those who were able to compare the industrial school classroom with an ordinary national school disputed this.

I went to regular schools so I can say they weren't party places either but they were light years away from this place. Nobody will ever know or be able to recreate the terror in those rooms—reigns of terror every day. It was horrendous.   *Bridget*

Control of information and the abuse of power

Research participants were deprived of information about their own life and family circumstances and this had a profound impact on their ability to concentrate and to learn. At times they were unaware of the reason for their placement in care. They were often discouraged from having contact with parents and not informed when their siblings were being moved to other institutions. This may have been because of age or gender or some other unexplained logistical factor.

For most survivors the sense of abandonment by their parents was a pain held silently and rarely articulated. Those who felt comfortable to talk about this aspect of their life several decades beforehand, were often still angry and distressed by what they had undergone.

It is very hard for me to understand why my mother, after we went into care, she never came to see us. It's even harder if you have known somebody. My very last recollection of my mother was her being in the court and me being stopped from going to her. She was there in the court but she never made any advance to me. So I think that most children if they had of been in care; if they had had any connection with their mother before they went into care that would have been harder on them. The bond would have been more severely damaged by the loss of their mother. I (pause) there is a saying 'what you don't have you don't miss' and I think in this context that could be true. But that doesn't say that that child doesn't need love from someone. I am one of the ones that didn't have any contact with their parents. But there was also the thing that you know if your mother came up and if the nuns didn't like your mother they were told not to bother coming again which meant that that child was deprived all the time.   *Jane*

Yeah, it [literacy] wasn't the thing that I was worried about. I was actually just worrying about when I was getting out and then I was thinking that I was going to be left there and I cried and cried and then I got to the stage where I didn't cry at all. I just accepted it and I wouldn't cry because there didn't seem to be any point in crying. Nobody hugged you. You actually got more trouble. You got into trouble for crying. I didn't cry.

Dara

My mother died when I was two and my father (pause) there was six of us in the family; we were all just one after the others. We were sent away. Just the boys stayed at home and the girls went into care? My father never took us out of the industrial school. Why I don't know. He very rarely came to see us either. I don't know what is the thing behind that. A lot of people were told that they shouldn't come and see us because it made us upset.

Tania

Whether children knew their parents or not, it is clear that the absence of a primary carer from their lives did make a major impact on every aspect of their well-being and was a desolate backdrop to their early learning. Sometimes siblings filled this gap but they too could inexplicably be taken away.

Derek described the sudden disappearance of his brother as a turning point in his literacy learning. Up until that point he was actually enjoying school and although 'the learning was a bit rough' he was happy and socially integrated and 'enjoying the interactive stuff.' Later in his narrative he explains his adult mistrust of groups and his inability to stay with any group learning process for any length of time. He is a loner who traces this trait to the betrayal and anger associated with his loss of his brother.

It is one of the main reasons why I do think that I couldn't read and write properly. When he was ten years old I was seven and when you reached ten years old you were taken away and put in another institution. And he was taken away at ten and I was left there.

Derek

Gus was a baby of three months when he first went into care with his older brother Simon. Again they were separated when Simon was moved to another institution and their only remaining family relationship was severed once and for all.

But even back then (pause) I mean when we were in (names institution) from 1969 and Simon was transferred to (names institution) and for years I didn't know where he was. It was like I dreamed I had a brother. But then I found out where he was. And that was it. But there was no relationship there because I never really knew him.   *Gus*

In every aspect of life, survivors were expected to obey without understanding and this demand for docility and obedience pervaded the learning situation. It produced submissive and subjugated children afraid to feel or to display any spark of enthusiasm for the cognitive process. For many this pattern has led to vulnerability and passivity in later life.

There are stories of survivors who would go to people's houses and they would think that they were going to their uncles but they were actually sent there to work. They never told them anything and so naturally enough, if that is your experience then you don't take part in any decision-making. You just go to where they tell you. You are not empowered to think for yourself.   *Centre worker*

Silence, secrecy and lies

Power was often wielded through silence and secrecy. Silence was the refuge of frightened learners and secrecy was the means of control used by abusers and those who were clearly aware of the shamefulness of their actions. In the first instance, for fear of being beaten, Vincent carried the secret of sexual abuse. Then silence became a form of internalised oppression that operated for forty-three years before he was finally able to unburden himself to his family.

And I know what happened to them behind closed doors and nobody seen what went on there. You couldn't tell the others what happened because you would get a beating. Forty-three years until I told my wife about that and I was scared to tell her and afraid to tell my children or anyone else. So eventually I had to get it out of me. Now they believe me and they trust me.   *Vincent*

Susie's sister had spent decades in a mental institution as a result of post-natal depression and more recently it had emerged that she was silenced about early childhood sexual abuse. She could not, or dared not speak out about being raped at the age of five by her mother's partner. Susie herself was aware that she was made complicit in secrecy around abuse in the classroom in industrial school and recognised that sometimes being silent was a negative, learned response. She was afraid to say what she knew in class for fear of punishment and at the same time she was silenced about wrongs committed by those in authority. This was both morally confusing and intellectually paralysing.

> I have to tell you that I experienced a nun beating a girl (pause). She asked her to do a sum on the board and she didn't know it and she was clattered on the back of the neck and she was unconscious. And the young girl was taken to hospital and the nun disappeared for a long time and we were told to keep our mouths shut and say nothing. And that fear (pause) and then the fear of not knowing—I can't explain. How could I explain this? I didn't answer in case I gave the wrong answer. I held back and I didn't give the answer.   *Susie*

Tania realised that her sister was removed from school and put to work before it was legally permissible to do so and that the process of so doing must have been covert and falsely recorded.

> My sister was kept back from school to work in the kitchen. Everyone but my sister went to school past eleven years of age. I don't think that she went to school because she was too stupid by that stage. She should have been in the industrial school until she was sixteen and they sent her to work when she was thirteen. That was against the law because the courts signed her in until she was sixteen. But of course that was all hidden.   *Tania*

Respondents constantly reminded me that these systemic injustices were actually perpetrated on children. Because it is always adults who now articulate the narratives of industrial schools, this was a significant issue to highlight. When adults voice childhood hurts, the total vulnerability of the child can easily be masked and forgotten.

Abuses of power

The Residential Institutions Redress Act (2002) identified four main types of abuse that took place in industrial and reformatory schools: sexual, physical and emotional abuse and neglect. With echoes of state harm as described by (Hillyard *et al.*, 2004) 'neglect' is defined in the Residential Institutions Redress Board Guide (2004: 12) as including 'failure to provide legally prescribed minimum of school instruction, lack of appropriate vocational training or training in life skills.' Furthermore the Act recognised that these abuses could cause physical or psychiatric injury and illness, psychological injury and loss of opportunity. Psychological injury included emotional hurts like: inability to show affection or trust; low self-esteem; literacy level well below capability and limited vocabulary leading to communication difficulties. An example of loss of opportunity was 'having to refuse employment opportunity/promotion because of illiteracy' (Residential Institutions Redress Board, 2004:14). Redress awards were made based on an assessment of the severity of the abuse and the injury suffered by applicants. The abuses described by respondents in this research did not always fit neatly into categories and it was evident that lack of care and attention to literacy was intricately enmeshed with other abuses although not always recognised as such.

Repeating patterns

There is evidence that the process of state neglect is repeating itself in the lives of survivors with unmet literacy needs. One solicitor feared that many survivors had not been fully informed about the detail of their own Redress case. Those who attended the hearings of the Commission to Inquire into Child Abuse felt that there was no effort made in the later hearings to include survivors and make information accessible and not solely reliant on text. Some suggested that survivors were not given information about schedules of meetings and their requests for clarification of legal detail was treated with irritation and this in a process where they are of central importance as expert witnesses on their own lives. A counsellor with wide experience of working with survivors asserted that the Irish State had not made enough effort in its Redress process to accommodate those with unmet literacy needs. In Canada and Australia where similar inquiries into institutional abuse have taken place, the unmet literacy needs of survivors have been discussed in the context of creating a process that was transparent, accessible and inclusive (Graycar and Wangmann, 2007).

Failure to do this in Ireland may mean that some survivors were deprived of redress all together.

> If Redress had got its message out to people; if it had made videos; if it had made recordings and moved to being accessible to people, maybe there would be many thousands more. There was every effort to do something but not too much, to keep the lid on and not open it too much. *Counsellor*

In the experience of those with unmet literacy needs who attended the Redress Board, it did not always deliver the intended satisfactory sense of closure or systemic reparation. Jim described the process like a form of recurring paedophilia where a familiar abusive pattern is repeated. Individuals were taken behind closed doors, relived their abuse, were given money and forbidden to speak any further about their experiences. In addition to this clear resonance, literacy matters also were treated with the same indifference as in the past and many were left with a sense that they and their education were of little value and their unmet literacy needs were of little consequence.

The legal professionals interviewed also expressed this opinion that illiteracy was not fully understood by the Redress Board.

> I have yet to see anyone who got a decent award on loss of opportunities and yet they can prove that they were in [industrial school] for the whole of their life up until sixteen and didn't sit any exams and didn't learn to read or write.   *Legal professional*

Another solicitor suggested that this attitude to literacy might be an idea 'born out of an accountant's mind' whose interest lay in reducing payments by the fifteen per cent allowed for *loss of opportunity*. It may equally be rooted in a belief implied above that a family of origin, rather than the education system, determined learning outcomes. Those who accompanied survivors through the Redress process felt that it was difficult to get the Redress Board to acknowledge the real, serious harm that had been done by unmet literacy needs. It was also difficult to establish that the failure did not lie with the individual or his or her perceived cultural expectations.

They say it all the time. All the misfortunes that befell somebody during the course of their lives were predictable because of circumstances of a secular predetermination.   *Legal professional*

Empathy is an integral part of care and those who have no direct experience of illiteracy struggled to even understand such levels of educational deficit. This was further aggravated by selectivity about the voices that were valued and a preference for evidence of measurable abuses.

Generally there would be a role for an educational psychologist. They [the Redress Board] like doctors and they don't have a lot of time for anyone else. So you better not send in any real professionals. Psychologists are down the line and the counsellor is way, way down the line even though you may have been attending the counsellor for the last six years and that would be the person who knows you best. It is a very old-fashioned approach. They are all middle-class people that went to the top schools. It is a boarders' convention of the doctors and the lawyers. *Legal professional*

Unmet literacy needs were a primary motivation in the request for the establishment of the Education Fund and the Lighthouse Centre for adult education. Nevertheless this value is not reflected in the way that literacy was considered by the Redress Board which continued to reflect the low expectations and past patterns of inequality of the industrial school system. Those whose literacy levels meant that they were unable to prepare or independently read the Redress Board documentation felt marginalised and powerless. Many had expectations of justice that were ultimately disappointed.

Sexual abuse

One man said, because of the prevalence of maltreatment, it was as if those employed in industrial schools had 'been given the green light' by the system to sexually abuse children in their care. Not all members of staff were abusers but those that were, dominated and silenced not only the children they molested but also their colleagues, who became complicit through their silence and implied acquiescence.

One man remembered his delight when the industrial schools were closed and in the late 1980s he was moved to a 'family unit'. Here also he was abused. His hopes were dashed and he felt utterly alienated by the 'sick home' that this new site of sexual abuse represented. The failure to adequately regulate such care homes made it possible for paedophiles to gain employment as carers and to groom and assault children unchecked by the system. In the industrial school, fear of sexual abuse was a dominant concern and often meant lack of sleep and at best, the feelings of guilt at wishing the abuse would be visited on someone other than you. These environments were not conducive to learning.

> It was the fear. The nights that I prayed that your man would go and pick somebody else out of their bed. Nightly—with more than one fellow. I prayed every night … That they passed my bed. Swear to God. And that makes you feel terrible guilty.   *Paul*

Physical abuse

Children in industrial schools were frequently beaten. The severity of the punishment ranged from corporal punishment, like that sanctioned in the mainstream education system of the time, to serious physical assaults that resulted in hospitalisation. A number of survivors in the Lighthouse Centre bore scars and permanent physical disabilities from their days in industrial school and I was repeatedly told many of these stories in the course of my research. Any literacy learning took place under a constant threat of physical punishment that was cognitively counterproductive and emotionally destructive. Physical abuse was always accompanied by verbal taunts that denigrated the individual, demonised their identity and paralysed their capacity to absorb new information or skills. No allowance was made for individual learning need, style or pace. Every respondent described being slapped, beaten and 'clattered around the ears' as part of the literacy learning process. A disproportionate number of the clients in the Lighthouse Centre had hearing difficulties that they attributed to these beatings.

The constant but unpredictable practice of physical abuse preoccupied most children who were then unable to make progress with literacy.

> I became more and more withdrawn in class. I could read and write a bit but I was afraid to answer a question in case I got a clatter. It didn't matter if you knew the answer or not. There was no logic. You would be sitting in class and you have all these rows of desks. They would be walking up and down and checking your work and then suddenly you

get a slap across the head and you wouldn't know what you were getting
it for.   *Susie*

Kevin was seven when he went into care and became fearful of learning.

I didn't like the school there. I hated it. There was a terrible tense
atmosphere. And like you would be looking at them to see if they were
in a bad mood. There was always somebody getting a right beating. And
you were tense all through the class and afraid. If you got something to
do you would be scared. I didn't like it—it was too tense.   *Kevin*

The punishments were obviously painful but the name-calling and emotional
devastation of being constantly attacked was also wearing for children. Bridget
was literate when she went to the industrial school but remembered that others
were often beaten for not knowing how to read or spell words. In the punishing
environment of the institution, as time went by, she felt her own skills regress.

And I remember that they used to get their hands beaten off with rulers.
I will tell you what I do want to say. The longer I was in the environment
the less I excelled. I knew I was capable of much more.   *Bridget*

Tania was amongst a small minority who suspected that they might have
learned as a way of avoiding being beaten. Her account suggested that she
learned despite, rather than because of the regime.

I don't remember learning to read. We never had books only the
schoolbooks in the industrial school. I suppose I learned from them.
Now whether I learnt to read and write out of fear, I don't know. Learnt
to read and write instead of getting beaten. It is another way of looking
at it. I was going to excel in that instead of being beaten. I hated being
smacked you know. I hated it. I suppose I wanted to stop the beating so
I went that way.   *Tania*

Some men remembered being stripped and beaten in front of their peers,
ostensibly because of a failure to carry out a literacy act as requested, but actually
as an excuse for abusing them sexually as well as physically. Martin saw the
physical abuse as an inherent part of the wider policy of domestication. Matt

saw punishment as a refuge from ineptitude on the part of teachers who were unable to manage the dynamics of learning within their classroom.

> In those classes—which were completely different from my first school—there was kind of a form of anarchy because the teacher was as bad and maybe the cause of it all. But it was coming from the boys as well and I think it was coming from the uneven learning or knowledge of the different boys. It was like topsy-turvy and then the way that they used to conduct themselves in the class—the Brothers. One guy might not know the question and he would be really punished. There were a lot of boys getting punished.   *Matt*

The premeditation and sadistic quality of the corporal punishment was clear in the detailed preparation that was put into the implements of punishment by Gary's teacher.

> He had a variety of leather straps and canes and all of these implements. He used to get me to boil the leathers with cod liver oil or something like that to stop them from fraying. And then another time he got me and a friend of mine, who died on the streets a couple of years ago, he used to get us to break the ends of the bamboo so that they would splinter. New canes had to be splintered so that they would inflict maximum pain and they would shoot splinters into your arm. And then as well as that he had the odd leg of a table, leg of a chair and he would get us to tape them up because it would frequently wear out—he couldn't get a grip on it. That was if you did something really bad.   *Gary*

This type of detail was reflected in the published hearings of both male and female witnesses to the Commission to Inquire into Child Abuse (2003). The report cited lengthy lists of instruments used to beat children. The implication of some children in the preparation of the weapons of punishment provided an additional and sinister factor.

Emotional abuse

Examples of emotional abuse given by the Redress Board are:
> Depersonalisation e.g. through family ties being severed without justification or through deprivation of affection.

General climate of fear and apprehension.

Stigmatisation by staff, through repeated racist remarks or hurtful references to parents (Residential Institutions Redress Board, 2004).

Each of these examples emerged in this empirical study and was often cited as having a direct impact on literacy learning. In fact, it is impossible to imagine the threat and practice of sexual and physical abuse existing separately from their emotional consequences. Even those who did not directly experience extremes of abuse in industrial schools, were emotionally damaged, simply by being present in that threatening place. Carol described to me how she taught herself not to cry with such efficacy that she is still unable to do so aged fifty-one. A worker in the centre attributes the serious emotional damage not just to the harmful acts that took place but also to the relentless nature of the abusive environment from which there was no respite.

> I think what makes people that were in institutions different is that there wasn't respite. If somebody was in the care of a particular institution or order or organisation for the majority of their childhood they didn't have anywhere else. If you are a child who is terribly bullied at school or abused at home then maybe there is some respite at home or in school and in institutions you don't get that.   *Centre worker*

Systemic neglect allowed the industrial schools to operate until the late1980s and there is considerable evidence that abuse and educational inequality, particularly for disadvantaged children, did not end when they closed (Department of Education and Skills, 2004).

Neglect by the state

Departmental inspections did take place in some schools but the descriptions graphically illustrate how cosmetic these were. One woman said this was the only day when resources were produced and the staff 'projected their own fears onto the children and made them nervous wrecks'. As adults who were constantly reflecting on the past, survivors failed to understand how such atrocities as they experienced were allowed to go unchecked.

> It is something I will always have in my mind. And always think and always look for reasons and searching and asking how could they not monitor what was going on? How did the state not know what was

going on? Why were there not more social workers knocking around? Why was there nobody? Why could these people get away with it? *Bob*

Respondents repeatedly identified the provision of literacy education as the responsibility of the Department of Education, on behalf of the state. As Sara remarked:

> Children have a right to an education no matter what background they are from.
>
> *Sara*

Through a process of community politicisation, survivors have become acutely aware of educational inequalities that were unclear to them as children. Tania's sister, who is still unable to read and write today, was actually removed from school to work full time in the kitchens. She felt that this should have been evident from school records and queried, as should the low progression routes from institutions to higher levels of education.

> And the Department of Education has a big part to play in it because they didn't have representatives coming into industrial schools and seeing what was going on. You know hardly any of us went on to third level education or even to secondary school. Surely they can't have thought we were all stupid. It must have been on record that my sister wasn't going to school at that time. They are all to blame—the Department of Education inspectors.
>
> *Tania*

Both Susie and Pam were clear that they had been denied a basic educational right through state neglect and through unequal allocations of state care.

> It was the government's responsibility to see that everyone got their absolute entitlement and it was their entitlement to learn how to read and write.
>
> *Susie*

> I would say the government should have been more careful. There would have been children where I was that wouldn't have been able to read and write. But they were just kind of pushed to one side.
>
> *Pam*

Failure to ensure that children's basic educational needs were met was construed by survivors as a measure of the degree of neglect they suffered.

Outcomes of power abuses—Institutionalisation

Carl did not come into the Lighthouse Centre very often but asked to come in one day to talk to me. He had a lot of memory blanks about his childhood in care that he attributed to medication he took for depression. He did not remember learning to read and write and assumed that the process was fairly unproblematic for him. He was confident about his literacy skills and an avid reader. He was one of five children and went into care when he was three. His father was blind and his mother was often hospitalised but he remembered that she visited them often up until her death. Retrospectively, he reasoned that both children and staff were part of an institutionalised regime that suffered from what Shield calls an absence of *knowledgeable* care (Shield, 2006: 26).

> You might have got a few slaps or whatever but like I wouldn't hate them. I would feel sorry for them. I think they were probably institutionalised as well. Some of the women had had babies and they were there for their whole lives—institutionalised—that's the surroundings. I mean in those days there was no professional training. The religious kind of run all the places and the government would have kept handing the money over, you know.
> *Carl*

Many men headed for the army as a natural progression from their regimented upbringing. Here, their unmet literacy needs constrained their prospects of promotion and ensured they remained in the most powerless lowest ranks.

> So they went from one institution to another and then taking on the army life, they would accept the discipline. Very significant numbers would have emotional problems—therefore heavy drinking or fighting—but some made tremendous soldiers. The one thing that was missing was literacy so they could function as squaddies but go no further up the ranks. They were made for obedience.
> *Counsellor*

As a community, survivors of abuse in industrial schools struggled against recreating another institutional regime. They drew a distinction between making rules and helping people become socialised in ways that they may have missed through being institutionalised and regimented in childhood. This vigilance involved much dialogue about the fine line between authoritarianism and democracy.

Outcomes of power abuses—Internalisation of abuse

The consequences of an abusive learning culture continued to impede literacy learning in adult life. One woman in her early 60s spoke in a child's voice and rocked in her seat for the first few weeks that we worked together. She had no recollection of ever being in school and what little literacy she had was learned from a woman with whom she was placed in service when she was a teenager. When I worked with her she was a more contented adult learner but would still hit herself viciously when she made an error or forgot a word in the passage she was reading.

Others displayed their long memories in almost imperceptible but ever-present responses. They winced at sudden movements, closed doors, loud noises or someone approaching from behind. Literacy tutors were constantly patrolling the borders between past and present, deflecting and disarming negative echoes and substituting positive learning experiences.

> I don't like when people are behind me after all the bad things that came from behind. Frightened still to go to the toilet.   *Paul*

Carol and Brenda described how they internalised the dogma of domination and turned it upon themselves and others. Brenda remembered as a child being alone and thirsty yet knowing she must not turn on a tap. Carol disclosed how she regulated the boys in her care with a brutality that was not part of her nature. In the Lighthouse Centre, one day I came across a fifty year-old woman sobbing like a child. She told me that her literacy tutor was unhappy with her work and she felt frightened and emotionally transported back to her school days. In actual fact it emerged that a tutor had drawn an arrow across her work to indicate where she should reposition something she had written. She had seen this as her work being scored out and felt immediately worthless and fearful of punishment.

Resistance—then and now

Inevitably children managed the institutional regime in different ways depending on their personality, level of support and in some cases physical strength.

> I was fourteen but I wasn't supposed to be put out until I was sixteen. I
> just rebelled so much that when I got a bit heavier in myself; when I got
> to the stage where I was fed up being hit I just lost control of my body
> and broke a bottle and brought it to his head and said, 'never again are
> you going to hit me'. And within a week I was out.   *Bill*

Others talked of becoming hard-skinned both literally and metaphorically.
Some boys pragmatically toughened their hands against beating by playing
handball. Others encased themselves in protective shells that isolated them from
the worst impact of the harsh regime. Derek, who was fifty-two, had discovered
through his personal research that thirty of the seventy boys who were in his
age group in the industrial school were already dead. He said, 'they just gave up'.
  On reflection, Tania thought that learning became a form of resistance for
her that enabled her not only to survive but also to pass on a love of learning
to her children.

> I don't know why education meant so much to me. Maybe it was a form
> of retaliation for me. Now why I rebelled against being told I was stupid
> I don't know. My sister didn't rebel against it and maybe that is why she
> never learnt and maybe that is why she began to believe that she was
> totally stupid. I loved to learn. My older lad had the same thing. He
> loved to learn. He picked it up from me. Education is power mum. You
> have the education—you have the power. You can do anything. *Tania*

Gary missed out on literacy and spent time on the streets as a homeless person
with alcohol addiction. At the time of the study, he was a playwright and actor
and had found a way of using his childhood experiences creatively.

> You don't have time for learning so you don't have time to become a good
> student at anything but you do become a survivor and a good student
> of life. So you watch people and you take cues from people as you grow
> up and the cues that you get confirm whether you are doing okay or not.
> And even to this day as an actor I put it into my work because it gives
> me an edge. It gives me a raw edge on actors who haven't had the same
> background as me (pause). For instance, if I have to play a gangster, I'm
> really convincing.   *Gary*

Breaking silence

Layers of silence and secrecy hung over people until the truth about abuses in industrial schools finally began to emerge toward the end of the 1990s. Secrets about having been in state care, about various forms of abuse and about illiteracy, have all been gradually brought out into the open and this is good for everyone. Speaking out in solidarity about institutional abuse finally broke the stranglehold of secrecy. In many ways, this ethnographic study added another opportunity for survivors to make sense of the past and to retell their stories.

> And they don't have to think they are dirty or it is their fault. The more and more it became known what happened in institutions, the more and more people came forward.
>
> *Carol*

From being isolated and subjugated by silence, survivors had found a new sense of community and a way of reaching out and connecting with others. They had lifted the veil on the insular repressive silence of the past.

Conclusions

The research data about the care/power interface gathered from those who were resident in industrial schools confirmed that they were traumatised in many ways by the excessively authoritarian regime they experienced in State care. They were not given clear and honest information about their circumstances and many did not understand why they had been abandoned by their parents. This induced a loss of identity, motivation and hope about the process of learning.

Many of those from industrial schools ended up with serious addictions, living on the streets or died prematurely. Others struggled throughout their lives to manage the consequences of damage done to them in care. The power wielded over those consigned to these schools was intended to subjugate them as servants within an hierarchical state that was strongly influenced by authoritarian religious doctrine and church dominated organisations. It was believed that children needed to be disciplined and controlled for their own benefit, as well as for the wider good of the state. Care in general, and learning care in particular, was not seen as part of this process that was consciously harsh and controlling and designed to domesticate rather than educate. Control then spilled over into abuses that generated levels of fear and dread that overshadowed everything else.

Children were regularly victims of some form of abuse and their most basic needs were neglected, including the need to be literate and to develop their capabilities. Authoritarian excesses allowed brutalities to become commonplace and the state failed to fulfil its duty of care by allowing these abuses to remain secret and to go unchecked. The empirical data lists examples of systemic neglect, lack of regulation, inspection and attention to the quality of life of those in care either by the state or by the host religious orders. Even those who were not directly involved in abusing children became complicit by their silence.

At its most extreme, the absence of care in the industrial school system was expressed in the threat and performance of acts of emotional, psychological, physical and sexual domination. All of these inevitably impinged on the learning environment in one way or another. Either they took place in the classroom and were directly related to the process of learning literacy, or their impact was so overwhelming that concerns of self-preservation put literacy beyond reach. In an atmosphere of constant fear and with a mechanistic approach to learning, literacy was at best a fragile oasis in a barren landscape. More often it was associated with physical punishment and terror and another means of producing a docile, obedient underclass. In industrial schools, for the most part, harm totally eclipsed care.

Chapter 7

Learning care lessons

The whole thing about our childhood was to keep us down. Education was too good, too powerful for us. If we had been able to read and write we would have become stronger; but by keeping us down we were vulnerable and they could abuse us.   (Tania)

Introduction

Tania's words illustrate the uplifting potential of learning and the vulnerability and oppression felt by many adults excluded from literacy use today and in the past. Access to what Crowther *et al.*, (2001: 1-9) have termed 'powerful literacies', emerged from this ethnographic study as inextricably linked to matters in the affective domain—to love, care and solidarity. This is not news. Current adult literacy learners constantly remind us about the importance of relational aspects of the learning process, yet these affective issues have received relatively little academic or pedagogical attention. Similarly, the harm caused by persistent state neglect of some sections of society is also obfuscated by discourses of school and family inadequacy. Now, more than ever, as the drive for accreditation, productivity and performativity in the field of adult literacy accelerates, we need to learn more about care as resistance, as well as a pivotal element in pedagogical praxis (O'Brien, 2008; 2011). This naming of care and beginning to unpick the role that it plays in supporting literacy learning is part of a process of recognising and professionalising affective elements of teaching and learning.

We know that across social contexts the complex role of care is often unrecognised, undervalued and overshadowed by economic concerns (Engster, 2004; 2007; Gheaus, 2009; 2013; Lynch *et al.*, 2009). So too, affective aspects of teaching and learning have been perceived as a natural, often gendered phenomenon, for which no additional training or resources are necessary (Gannerud, 2001). In the specific instance of adult literacy, Freirean emphasis on issues of power in the learning relationship was evident—at least before neo-liberal imperatives intervened (Freire, 1972; 1994; 1997; 2001). Here, the concept of *learning care* includes and moves beyond power to describe learning relationships situated in a multidimensional definition of equality. As such, learning care focuses more comprehensively on the interwoven strands of power, status and resources in learning relationships as they operate in the private, public and civic sectors. Ultimately each type of learning care described below is shown to depend on the degree to which it is enabled by effective exercise of the state duty of care.

This final chapter draws together the conclusions about learning care from the ethnographic study and elaborates the four-part model of learning care that has emerged. For each type of learning care, some relevant contemporary literacy issues are indicated that bring up to date the reflections about past literacy inequalities.

Despite general neglect, recognition is growing across the educational spectrum that affective matters are an important part of how and what we learn. We have explored in chapter three how studies have begun to focus on a range of affective issues such as: care and the school curriculum (Cohen, 2006; McClave, 2005); teachers' emotional labour (Hargreaves, 2000; 2001); the role of the affective domain in educational ideology (Lynch *et al.*, 2007; Lynch *et al.*, 2009); a school ethic of care (Noddings, 1992; 2006; 2007) mothers' care labour in children's education (O'Brien, 2005; 2007; Reay, 2000) and 'children's vision of their care worlds' (Luttrell, 2013: 1). Each of these authors has taken some vital perspective on affective elements of teaching and learning and placed it more prominently on the educational agenda. Adding in another dimension, this study took a *literacy turn* to examine the arguments about the relationship between literacy and care in/equalities. Coining the concept of 'learning care', based on the empirical findings, I propose that affective dimensions of equality are pivotal and powerful in establishing more just literacy outcomes (Feeley, 2009; 2010; 2012). My hope is that a focus on in/equalities of care will bring a fresh perspective for all of us concerned with literacy matters and working for greater educational justice.

Literacy, care and social justice

New Literacy Studies have convincingly highlighted the need to contextualise literacy (Barton and Hamilton, 1998; Barton *et al.*, 2000; Giroux, 1987; Hamilton, 1998; Kress and Leeuwen, 1996; Street, 2001). If we accept that literacy is socially situated and a tool in the movement for social justice (Freire, 1972), then more fully understanding the unequal nature of that social backdrop is a necessary part of that struggle. An equality perspective (Baker *et al.*, 2004; 2009) provided a conceptual base for this study from which to examine aspects of the wider, hegemonic social context in which literacy and care were located. An equality framework allowed the complex weave of in/equality to be somewhat untangled and this helped identify and explore the strands of the literacy/care context. The data provided evidence of learning care determined by resources (chapter four), respect and recognition (chapter five) and power (chapter six) in the lives of survivors of abuse in Irish industrial schools. It became clear that in the Spartan environment of the institutions even small advantages were enabling and improved the chance of positive literacy outcomes. A used exercise book from a more privileged child, even minimal contact with a family member and small, respectful kindnesses from an individual teacher were all remembered as positive learning influences in a generally negative environment. Similarly, deprivation, discrimination and abuses of power were impediments to care that negatively impacted on literacy learning. Each dimension of equality was significant in the way that it had a determining influence on levels of care and care itself was pivotal in literacy learning. Reports from other locations where literacy and institutional abuse have been linked suggest that the Irish experience is by no means unique. Disadvantaged children, including aboriginal children were similarly treated in the care of the state (and religious groups) in the USA (Oates, 1995), Australia and Canada (Coldrey, 1993; 1999; Greycar and Wangmann, 2007), Northern Ireland and Scotland (Raftery and O'Sullivan, 1999)[17.]

The centrality of care

The findings of this ethnographic study have indicated a model of learning care, in the context of literacy, which builds on the work of Kathleen Lynch (2007). She proposed a model of three concentric circles of care relations—primary, secondary and tertiary contexts where care is both given and received. Each level of care is associated with a form of work: love labour in primary care relations, care work in secondary care relations and the collaborative agency involved in solidary activity.

---

17. In Canada, New Zealand, Australia and elsewhere there are similar accounts of aboriginal and marginalised people being taken into institutions where they were subjected to authoritarian regimes and extreme attempts to erase their cultural identity. A repressive regime of discipline and punishment like that described by Foucault (1975) was commonplace in many educational establishments in the first half of the twentieth century and was further intensified in institutions that were ironically part of the 'care' apparatus of the state.

Figure 7.1: Learning care model

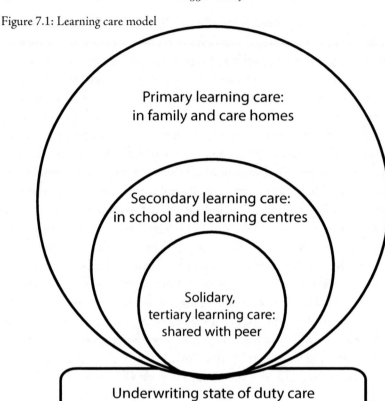

Primary learning care:
in family and care homes

Secondary learning care:
in school and learning centres

Solidary,
tertiary learning care:
shared with peer

Underwriting state of duty care

To be meaningful, care has to move beyond sentiment, attitude and intent to become realised in effort and actions that aim to benefit care recipients. Care is also work. This equally holds true for the notion of learning care. Located within the generic circles of care, learning care refers specifically to the impact of degrees of care on our capacity to absorb and retain new knowledge and skills. Being cared for, in a general way, allows us to enter hopefully and confidently into learning situations. Then within the generic circles of care there are specific attentions and actions aimed at supporting and encouraging learning.

Building on Lynch's model (2007), in the context of literacy learning the three spheres of generic affection and action outlined previously in *Figure 3.1* (p. 60)are applied to the context of learning and illustrated in *Figure 7.1* with the underwriting state duty of care for all learners. These care links do not exist separately but have a symbiotic relationship, one with the other, where even small advantages impact positively on learner outcomes.

A cycle of neglect and harm

Abuse, neglect and harm are the antithesis of care and affection. For those who experienced abuse in Irish industrial schools the *dynamic cycle of learning care* elaborated in chapter three was reversed to become a *vicious cycle of neglect* illustrated below in *Figure 7.2*. Imbued with interconnected inequalities of resources, power, respect and recognition, the net result of this vicious cycle was one of harmed life chances and wasted potential (Hillyard *et al.*, 2004). Participants cited examples of extremes of poverty, powerlessness and misrecognition as contributory factors in their exclusion from learning.

Figure 7.2: A vicious cycle of neglect

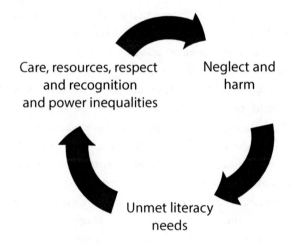

Care, resources, respect and recognition and power inequalities

Neglect and harm

Unmet literacy needs

Among the survivors of institutional abuse the results of neglect were evident in educational under-attainment, high unemployment, poor health, difficulty in making and sustaining relationships, high levels of dependency on alcohol and other harmful substances, extremes of psychological and emotional damage and high instances of suicide and premature death. A contributory factor in much of this legacy was the pervasive impact of stigmatising low levels of literacy. The data suggest that where even small privileging differences were brought to bear the negative cycle was counterbalanced by the hope of learning.

In this study, the contention therefore is that, imbricated with other chronic inequalities, people's unmet literacy needs were the product of ineffective and inequitable learning relationships. Where the positive affective factors that support learning were replaced with harmful and abusive attitudes and behaviours, all forms of flourishing were stifled. With primary care supports removed and solidary activities prohibited, survivors described withdrawing and becoming unreceptive to learning that was couched in threats of violence and humiliation. Ultimately, the state failed in its duty of care for vulnerable families and in its regulation of its own institutions and schools. Furthermore, an understanding of the nature of interconnected learning care inequalities for the critical case sample in this study allows us to better understand the roots of persistent literacy inequalities today. The pivotal factor is not that people are poor, excluded and powerless but that they are also consequentially deprived of care across the contexts where learning care has its influence. Contemporary learning care abuses and harms may be less culturally conspicuous than those of the past yet starkly unequal educational and life outcomes persist today and parallels can be drawn in the contemporary fields of childhood and adult literacy. These are discussed below for each strand of learning care.

The process and outcome of literacy acts and events, and learning how to participate in them, is almost always social and relational. Nevertheless, until recently, learning to read and write has been viewed as a purely cognitive matter (Lankshear and Knobel, 2003). As construed here, learning care describes the affective attitudes, emotions and actions, both paid and unpaid, that dynamically influence individuals and groups in learning literacy. Learning care is both given and received. It involves caregivers and recipients and these relationships are reciprocal (Feeley, 2009; 2010; 2012). The affective aspects of supporting and facilitating language and literacy development involve skill, effort and insight that cannot be taken for granted in the natural repertoire of every parent, teacher or tutor. As such, relational aspects of literacy facilitation need to be learned, practised and developed.

The history of survivors of institutional abuse is a harsh reminder that not everyone in society profits equally from care-giving. This in turn has a knock-on effect on many aspects of learning that care encourages and sustains, including literacy. This ethnographic research with survivors of institutional abuse in Irish industrial schools, suggested four discreet but interconnected sites and sources of learning care each with a distinct and combined relevance to the field of adult literacy today.

A model of learning care: Four types of learning care relationships

Four types of learning care are outlined below. In the first instance each one is briefly explained and then subsequently further elaborated in relation to the research data and contemporary issues in adult literacy.

1. *Primary learning care* in loving relationships is experienced within the family or an alternative primary care centre. As learning care recipients, this is true for children, young people and adults who benefit from the support and encouragement that facilitate learning. In adult literacy, inequalities in the skills and knowledge needed for primary learning care work are recognised in the attention now given to family literacy. Courses aim to enable and resource parents to support children's language and literacy development and interrupt cycles of educational disadvantage.

2. *Secondary learning care* occurs in caring relationships in schools, colleges and other places of adult learning. Mindfulness of learners' literacy needs is no longer confined to primary schooling. The need for ongoing support with traditional and new literacies is becoming widely recognised and the case for a relational emphasis in embedded or integrated approaches to literacy in all sectors has been well made (Hegarty and Feeley, 2009; National Research and Development Council, 2005). The National Research and Development Council study into the effectiveness of embedded or integrated approaches to language and literacy development in the UK found that the most important factor in all seven projects studied was the quality of the learning relationship (National Research and Development Council, 2005).

3. *Solidary learning care* is often experienced informally, in solidarity with peer learners and communities of interest, like the Lighthouse Centre where this study took place. Much adult literacy work includes and exemplifies a collaborative approach to learning where learners encourage and support each other in language and literacy development and practice. The Irish National Adult Literacy Agency (NALA) Learners' Forum is an example of how solidary learning care can be resourced and facilitated and learners empowered to become literacy activists (Cox, 2010). Other examples of critical, collaborative literacy, solidary learning care as resistance and praxis, exist around the world in groups that have experienced disadvantage. Supporting teachers and tutors in ways to enable and manage group approaches to learning are important. So too are opportunities for skills exchange and participation in learner events, social networks and online forums.

4. *State learning care* is defined here as the degree of attentiveness given by the state to ensuring structural equality (equality of condition) across all the contexts that influence family, school and community capacity to support literacy learning. This is a weak link in the learning care chain. Evidence of an absence of state learning care is apparent in persistent social and educational inequalities and the dearth of real solutions in terms of legislation and policy that moves towards equality of condition. The correlation between literacy outcomes and national measures of in/equality, measured in terms of the gap between low and high earners, potently illustrates this case (Wilkinson and Pickett, 2009). More equal countries constantly have better literacy outcomes than do those that are unequal.

Primary learning care

In its most intimate form, primary care relations encompass an interest in the well-being of the whole person and this includes support for their learning needs. All parents want the best for their children yet the love labour devoted to supporting literacy is dependent on many factors that are resource, status and power-related.

Those, like Carol, who had memories of learning care at home, carried the positive influence with them through the dark days in the institution. The empirical evidence suggested a largely affective component in the way that people learned about the importance of literacy as well as in the literacy learning process itself. There was no doubt that this relational impact began very early in life and the findings suggested that the ease with which one became literate was intricately linked to the presence of a secure affective base. That security was influenced by a family's position in terms of resources, status and power.

Some respondents had no experience of family life or the accompanying love labour that encompasses learning care. Those who had never known any home life were entirely dependent on the quality of care and learning in institutions and both of these was documented as abysmally poor. Children felt abandoned by parents and this isolation was exacerbated by the separation of siblings without explanation or warning. Derek, for example cited the sudden separation from his brother as an arresting point in his learning trajectory.

A Lighthouse Centre worker described an absence of primary learning care that continues to be an accepted feature of social care contexts today. He also observed, for those that were previously deprived of primary and secondary learning care, the hopeful, compensatory nature of adult education in the affective as well as the educational domain. This optimism was evident in adult literacy learners in the Centre who repeatedly spoke in positive terms of having become enabled to learn in a supportive environment.

For most people, the natural locus of primary learning care is undoubtedly the family or alternative care centre, where nurturing relationships encourage us to develop all our capabilities, including literacy. This is evident in the *Learning care* map of interviewees (Table 1, p.29), and in the narratives in the earlier chapters where the role of primary learning care emerges as decisive. Those survivors who had early or intermittent opportunities for care with their family of origin, or in occasional visits from a family member, were also most likely to have met literacy needs when leaving care. Similarly, of those who finished school with unmet literacy needs, most had no family life or consistent family relationship while in care. The conclusive trend was towards a strong link between the sense of identity and connection forged by continuity of primary care and positive learning outcomes.

The capacity of the respondents' families to offer care in the home was negatively influenced by extremes of poverty, the disrespect that comes from perceived moral inferiority and the powerlessness of those without privilege to challenge a rigidly authoritarian system. Where some degree of stability was possible in the home, and education valued and promoted, a positive experience of literacy could be traced back to an early age. This varied in degree according to the age a child went into care and was explicit in the case of siblings, like Brenda and her sisters who had varying amounts of home care before being institutionalised.

We have seen evidence of the low expectations that industrial schools had of the children in their care. They were being prepared for lives of service and obedience and the presence or absence of family influence, was defining. Those who were sustained in any affective family framework could be encouraged and motivated by that relationship or even the memory of it. People told me repeatedly that their childhood was stolen and it is clear that in some cases that theft caused irreparable damage. A dearth of affection made future adult relationships problematic for many. In the same way, negative learning relationships in childhood left behind chartless territory for later life. Adults struggled to learn literacy that is deeply associated with loveless or damaged relationships from their past. Outside the understanding culture of the Lighthouse, they were expected to move seamlessly into adult learning opportunities; to rapidly close the gap between themselves and those with a loving, secure family base and they were judged harshly for not so doing. When confronted with damaged adults, it is often forgotten that the original harm was done to small, vulnerable children. Failure to make the connection between literacy learning and the affective domain obfuscates the centrality of early learning as a part of primary loving relationships. Apart from the satisfaction of basic survival needs, early love labour is about the development of life skills in the young of the species and for human beings this includes language and literacy acquisition. Love and learning emerged from the memories of survivors as close counterparts.

Family literacy—learning about primary learning care today

The term family literacy is ambiguous. It may be used to refer to the way in which diverse families use literacy as well as to describe the programmes designed to support parents role in language and literacy development (National Adult Literacy Agency, 2004). There is an assumption that those who have had successful school and family experiences will know, or be able to access information about how to support the development of a child's language and literacy. For that reason, family literacy courses are designed for disadvantaged parents and their children and may be organised in association with local pre-school or primary school provision or through community development activity. The existence of family literacy programmes reflects the reality that literacy and its benefits are still unevenly distributed across social groups, that this has persistent generational implications and that educational disadvantage continues to run alongside wider social inequalities (National Economic and Social Forum, 2009; Wilkinson and Pickett, 2009). Important elements of primary learning care emerge in a study of the detrimental impacts of inequalities on whole populations. The study correlated low levels of literacy with high levels of inequality.

> Essential for early learning is a stimulating social environment. Babies and young children need to be in caring, responsive environments. They need to be talked to, loved and interacted with. They need opportunities to play, talk and explore their world, and they need to be encouraged within safe limits, rather than restricted in their activities or punished. All of these things are harder for parents and other caregivers to provide when they are poor, or stressed or unsupported. (Wilkinson and Pickett, 2009:111)

What most family literacy courses aim to do is give parents an understanding of the 'literate language' and conventions of the education system and skills in supporting their development. As such, courses address some of the disadvantages parents face. They can simultaneously support adult reading development and the immediate need to address language development with pre-school children. Parents learn new, more engaging ways to read to children and techniques for posing questions about characters and storylines in a way that develops skills needed for school (Heath, 1983). Family literacy courses, and more recently family literacy websites, give information about books and games that allow parents and children to enjoy vital aspects of primary learning care. Evidence suggests that all parents want the best for their children but may be uncertain about how best to deliver on those aspirations (Cregan, 2007; Hegarty and Feeley, 2010). Again this reminds us that learning care skills need to be learned and resourced.

The limitations of family literacy courses

What family literacy and the language and pre-literacy elements of some parenting courses achieve is not without merit. However, although they may change the cycle of educational disadvantage for some individuals, they do not tackle the fundamental inequalities that mean that some children experience more in-family 'brute luck' in terms of life chances than do others (Gheaus, 2009).

Nor can family literacy courses change the fact that the gap between vernacular language and the 'literate language' of school makes schooling culturally uncomfortable for many children and their parents (Cregan, 2007). When consulted about language system differences children showed an awareness of the hierarchy of linguistic codes and their social class implications. Negative attitudes towards school are reinforced by the sense of anger, confusion and alienation felt by those for whom 'literate language' is furthest away from their mother tongue (Mac Ruairc, 2004).

Primary learning care, like much care work, remains gendered and participants in most family literacy courses are in fact mothers. Canadian research and commentary collated by the Literacy Assistance Centre (2003) looked critically at the challenges of engaging fathers into primary learning work with children (Green, 2003) and the mounting pressures on disadvantaged mothers to become teachers as well as shouldering most of the burden of generic primary care (Smythe and Isserlis, 2003). In the UK also, the gendered nature of family literacy emerged from the literature as a major concern as does the need for school literacy to recognise and respect vernacular language realities rather than disregard them (National Research and Development Council, 2008).

Family literacy programmes initially grew from an understanding of the vital importance of early, pre-school years in childhood development and recognition of the diverse literacy practices within families (Taylor, 1983). Several decades later, with the fundamental resource, cultural and power inequalities unchanged, the same arguments and incentive for family literacy remain pertinent. A recent nationwide study in the UK found that by the age of three, children from disadvantaged backgrounds were already a year behind their more privileged peers in using the language of school (Centre for Longitudinal Studies, 2010). Contemporary US figures placed the language and literacy gap between privilege and disadvantage at one and half years in the life of a five or six year-old child.[18] The correlated role of parents in supporting children's learning is well researched and links are clearly made between parents' cultural capitals, capabilities and their capacity to support their children (Allat, 1993; O'Brien, 2005; 2007; Reay, 1998; 2000). The role of primary learning care is clearly not solely dependent on the willingness and capability of parents but on the wider enabling role of the state in reducing persistent levels of inequality.

Secondary learning care

Accounts of secondary learning care in the industrial school were replete with details of time spent in the tension and fear that accompanied the threat of aggression and harm. Within that learning environment, corporal punishment and public humiliation were commonplace. In the immediate context, learning was blocked by terror and concerns with self-protection and survival. In the longer term, the abuses that were experienced resulted in damaged self-esteem, negative associations with the learning process and an inevitable mistrust of teachers and authority figures.

In addition to the pervasive sense of angst, large classes were managed as batches with no allowance for different learning styles. Those who were left-handed were demonised and brutalised. Literacy teaching was militaristic and anyone unable to grasp reading and spelling through primarily auditory methods was additionally disadvantaged. In some cases children attended 'outside' school where they reported that they were constantly reminded of their inferiority.

18. *Irish Times*, Wednesday 29 September 2010, Page 3: Children from poorer backgrounds over a year behind in language skills, study finds: Discrepancy in exposure to reading and writing, by Alison Healy.

Within both 'inside' and 'outside' school, Irish Travellers, orphans, those of mixed race, those perceived as morally defective because their parents were unmarried and those with learning difficulties all attracted additional abuse and disparagement. An absence of primary care was used systematically and maliciously to explain and legitimate the withholding of secondary learning care. The lack of a positive school learning experience in turn made learning in adulthood more daunting, suggesting that the impact of poor secondary learning care as well as being immediate, may also be lifelong.

Secondary learning care in adult literacy

The study in the Lighthouse Centre provided much evidence about the need for care-full approaches to all aspects of the adult literacy learning process. A tutor's ability to adopt a facilitative and sensitive approach to group work gained added weight when learners' past experience had attuned them to the subtle expressions of negative aspects of power. One man remarked that 'sometimes as an adult you can feel that you are being left at the back of the class too'. It is hard for adults to unlearn their fearful learning patterns and secondary learning care takes on added significance in the adult literacy context. People displayed their long, often visceral, memories in almost imperceptible but ever-present embodied responses. They winced at sudden movements, closed doors, loud noises or someone approaching from behind. One woman persistently hit herself for making small errors in reading and spelling. As well as learning literacy, people were also learning about making new relationships with themselves, with others and with their past; tutors discovered the need to make room for this. Literacy tutors had to be constantly vigilant for the emergence of hurts from the past, guarding against opening old wounds and creating new, positive learning memories. In this, they were attentive to learners' real condition, holding in mind their sensitivities and mapping different and effective routes to good literacy outcomes. This was all about care. It was not just about attitude and intent but also about strategic action. Secondary learning care is less about sentiment and more about skilled, respectful learning facilitation. It accurately and insightfully recognises individual and group needs, provides appropriate resources and pursues empowering methodologies that support people to flourish. Secondary learning care is a challenging pedagogical matter.

Embedded/integrated literacy—secondary learning care in action

Evidence from rich countries demonstrates that there are still large numbers of young people and adults whose literacy capability remains relatively undeveloped after years of statutory schooling (CEC, 2008; OECD, 2009; OECD/Statistics Canada, 2005). These literacy inequalities, as in the days of the industrial schools, impact on those who are less-well resourced, respected and represented in society (Lynch and Baker, 2005). Compensatory attention to school-age literacy has been increasing over the past decades with policy initiatives providing additional resources, time, and smaller classes for those with lived experience of social disadvantage (Machin, 2006; NESF, 2009; Smyth and McCoy, 2009). In adult education and training, responsibility for filling the literacy gaps of earlier schooling is being assumed through an embedded or integrated approach to language and literacy development (Hegarty and Feeley, 2009; National Research and Development Council, 2005). At its best, this approach has the potential to exemplify a form of secondary learning care in attitude and action, in that it demonstrates concern for those who have missed out and takes on a focused pedagogical attentiveness to their needs.

It could be argued that not adopting an integrated or embedded approach to language and literacy amounts to care-lessness. Integrating literacy in all teaching and learning is not just practical but also a matter of social justice. Unlike the excesses of disregard in industrial schools, it strives to ensure that adult learning does not penalise individuals and groups who are less well prepared for learning. Adopting an integrated approach in adult learning implies recognition that without wider social equality, without equality of condition, the myth of equal educational opportunities and outcomes is unfounded (Lynch and Baker, 2005). Embedding literacy implies the presence of learning care in that it demands a conscious, skillfull facilitation of subject matter in order to address gaps and inequalities in prior learning. Those who embark on courses, at whatever level, without confidence in their use of academic language and literacy often carry with them the negative influence of the associated social and cultural stigma. As well as satisfying a pedagogical imperative, integrated literacy therefore also has a strong moral justification to right wrongs and omissions in past educational relationships (Rogers, 2005).

Secondary learning care is not just a matter for individual teachers. Proponents of an integrated approach suggest that caring for learners works best when, as Noddings has argued for education in general, an entire organisation adopts an ethos of care (Noddings, 1992; 2007). A whole organisation approach to embedding language and literacy has not only been shown to provide an effective means of simultaneously dealing with literacy, vocational and other learning needs. There are wider, whole system equity and efficiency arguments for an integrated approach that claim to improve retention and achievement, thereby raising individual, community and national skills and social and economic well-being (National Research and Development Council, 2005).

The limitations of integrated literacy

The treatment of survivors of institutional abuse was called 'care' and so we must remember that motive, experience and outcomes are all important in our judgements about how genuinely caring educational practices really are. The contemporary concept of integrating or embedding literacy arose alongside pressures for improved productivity and workplace performance. It was not motivated by concern about educational inequality and care for those left behind by the system (Wickert and McGuirk, 2005). Like all forms of learning relationship, literacy work is never neutral but infused in structure and content with the values and priorities of policy-makers, funders, governing bodies and individual practitioners (Freire, 1998; Baker *et al.*, 2004). In general, those who hold power in education, those with vested interests, tend to be conservative, or at best philanthropic in their outlook and disinclined to question or seek to change deeply rooted inequalities in the status quo (Duru-Bellat, 2008; Lynch, 1999). For this reason, although adult education like that carried out in the Lighthouse Centre, can and does function as a site of critical reflection and resistance, it is more often a process infused with the acceptance and reproduction of dominant cultural norms and levels of learning care are limited by this greater priority (Aronowitz and Giroux, 1993; hooks, 1994; 2003; McGivney, 2001).

Integrated literacy involves some of the attributes of learning care yet the literature suggests that it remains predominantly linked to the potential credential and economic outcomes for individuals and the economic system (Sticht, 2003; 2007). It does not deal with the fundamental causes of literacy inequalities and so these harms, like those in the primary learning care sector, are set to continue.

Redressing literacy inequalities presents stubborn political and resource issues that have shown themselves to be resilient to many of the initiatives tried over the years. David Barton (2005) warns of the danger to adult literacy work as shifts in policy begin to take attention (and funding) away from one of the most complex areas of adult education. He reminds us of the almost magical powers that were attributed to literacy when it was claimed to be the key to redressing a whole raft of social and economic disadvantages (Moser, 1999). This extravagant and baseless claim, rather like the ease with which industrial schools were to deal with problematic children, clouded the realities of stubborn social inequalities. It implied a simplicity and speed in repairing the social injustice signalled by unmet literacy needs that is far from the truth and is inevitably failing to produce the desired results.

Aside from the ideological issues, those charged with managing the complex processes of embedding literacy across whole organisations and into specific subject areas do not always feel they have the necessary skills to do so. Like those in industrial schools whose imperative was control rather than teaching, today's tutors may lack the skills to deliver 'knowledgeable' learning care (Shield, 2006: 26) when their priority is increased performativity.

The need to recognise the centrality of relational aspects of adult literacy teaching and learning also emerged in Australian studies. Balatti *et al.*, (2006) have argued for a change in the understanding of success in literacy away from 'a single economic bottom line' to a tripartite measure involving economics, social capital and community development (Ibid: 12). The study claimed that the vital and undervalued role of relationships in the learning process needed to be made explicit in the training of teachers. Balatti *et al.*, found that we need to know more about the pedagogical practices that enable the different forms of affective and relational development that in turn build trust and empower learners.

Like the primary learning care initiatives that underpin family literacy programmes, integrated or embedded approaches to literacy risk merely papering over the cracks and fall short of eradicating secondary learning care inequalities. Young people and adults continue to emerge from school and college education with unequal achievements. These are often unrelated to capability but rather caused by social inequalities and lower expectations that dictate that some are more cared for and about in the education system than are others. In a different guise, there is a repetition of old problems: lack of resources and investment in teacher training, a failure to recognise root inequalities and a protection of productivity and profit for the few over the general good.

Solidary learning care

More than half of the participants in the research had begun to learn literacy in adulthood. Primary and secondary learning care relationships provided a bridge back into learning. This was through successful adult relationships, the desire to make a positive contribution to children's lives, and the liberating personal counselling process established in the aftermath of the state apology to those abused while in its care. Positive experiences of care in adulthood enabled survivors to develop greater self-esteem, a more solid sense of identity and consequently renewed hope that learning literacy was possible. Survivors describe primary learning care in their adult relationships and family; secondary learning care with friends and in adult education courses and solidary learning care in the Lighthouse Centre or other community groups. The demonstration of remorse expressed in the apology to survivors was experienced as an act of state care that enabled people to move forward with healing and building a more hopeful future.

In the Lighthouse Centre, the sense of shared history and collective struggle for justice formed a bond for survivors of abuse in industrial schools. Care became a strategy that might overcome harm so that learning could happen. Institutional life had left little time or space for friendship or solidarity and group learning was not on the pedagogical menu. It was only in later life that survivors began to savour the benefits of community solidarity and the second chance it provided for learning literacy. As well as those whose return to learning was enabled by new relationships of primary care in adulthood, the bond that formed around a common experience of abuse and neglect had also been transformational in attracting people back to literacy.

Lighthouse Centre workers and survivors themselves recognised that collaborative approaches to learning took on added significance in the context of shared struggle. The Centre was expressly founded for the purpose of 'healing through learning' and this mission was displayed in the entrance hall and repeated frequently by centre users. The ethnographic study that is described here did much to facilitate reflection, discussion and analyses of the difficulty of learning in authoritarian, repressive environments and became part of processing memories and taking power and control over the present.

Adult literacy today—opportunities for solidary learning care

Examples of solidary literacy projects abound today in diverse communities of interest wherever adults struggle to overcome inequalities and past educational neglect and harm. Survivors of institutional abuse represent the extreme end of a continuum that stretches across socially disadvantaged communities in both wealthy and poorer countries across the globe. However not all literacy is emancipatory or rooted in Freirean principles of praxis. The assumption that literacy, solidarity and development are involved in an unproblematic relationship has been called in to question in a collection of literacy ethnographies in the development field (Street, 2001). The same may also be said to be true in literacy work that is made necessary by unequal development within wealthier countries and is sanctioned, and funded to provide only very limited literacy learning. What is certain is that many adults in literacy groups today, like survivors of institutional abuse, also had harrowing experiences in mainstream education (Bailey and Coleman, 1998). It is a relief for them to meet with others in a similar situation and much of what happens in solidary learning care situations, like the Lighthouse Centre, is about sharing and overcoming these painful histories.

Adult literacy populations include specific interest groups of individuals who bond together in common cause shared by people with unmet learning needs and the residual harm of other social neglect. Empathy, recognition of injustices done and relief at setting aside shame are all part of what underpins the new learning situation. The adult learners in the Lighthouse demonstrated that in solidarity, there is a powerful remedial quality in the face of even the most desperate situation. The solidary learning care present in many such groups is well documented: trade union learning groups in a number of countries (Hamilton and Hillier, 2006; Street and Lefstein, 2007) asylum seekers in the UK and Ireland (Baynham, 2006; Ward, 2002), community-based women's groups in Ireland and Scotland (Barr, 1999; McMinn, 2000), First Nation people in Canada (Gabriel, 2006; Laughlin and Leman, 2010), Maoiri in New Zealand (Bowl and Tobias, 2012), women with experience of violence in Canada (Horsman, 2000; 2004) men's sheds in Australia and elsewhere (Golding *et al.*, 2007) and Gypsies, Travellers and ethnic minorities in the US (Mc Caffrey, 2009; Powell, 1999). What all these groups (and many more) have in common is that they harness specific shared experiences of inequalities and enable learners to 'name their world' as the literacy component of a wider praxis (Friere and Macedo, 1987). The affective nature of that shared learning, exemplified by its absence from industrial schools, is cited by all as a central factor in allowing learning to take place.

Adult literacy varies in the degree to which it is really empowering. Research carried out on the impact of Ireland's National Adult literacy Agency's (NALA's) student development work over a three-year period (Cox, 2011) showed that individuals, local groups and the National Adult literacy Agency all benefited from the involvement of an autonomous student group in literacy advocacy and development. The group was not only solidary but also representative in that some members became part of the organisation's executive committee and so their influence extended beyond the group to a national literacy forum. The research showed that solidary learning groups benefit from resourcing and facilitation. This echoes Noddings' argument that an ethos of care in education requires learning from more knowledgeable others who model, allow practice, provide feedback and engage in dialogue about (learning) care (Noddings, 1992; 2006; 2007). Adult literacy tutors assume the role of group facilitators and so how best to enable solidary learning care relationships needs to be part of tutor training.

Some limitations of solidary learning care

Although literacy as a form of praxis has much merit, the neo-liberal influence in many parts of the globe has sidelined what seemed like a natural solidary element in adult literacy practice for decades (Hamilton and Hillier, 2006). Now the 'skills for life' agenda in the UK and similar centralising movements elsewhere have a tendency to individualise learner progress in the drive towards accreditation and progression. Concerns with outcomes, have limited the opportunities, time and resources for critical, solidary learning that can, like association between children in industrial schools, be viewed as outside the agenda and against the interests of those in authority. A performativity culture has become increasingly preoccupied with learning expressed as numerical evidence and results. This in turn sidelines any interest in the affective nature of the learning process and marginalises resistance and collaboration (Ball, 2010). As was the case in industrial schools, care continues to be squeezed out by the concerns of capital and the status quo (Lynch *et al.*, 2009).

State learning care

The majority of the research participants (sixty-eight percent) asserted that the state neglected its direct responsibility to monitor the quality of care and education offered to them as children. Respondents described feelings of abandonment that transcended their immediate family and extended to the wider population. They saw an irony in the fact that they were taken away from families who were perceived to be unfit to offer care and supervision, only to be more grossly neglected in the alternative state provision.

Many attributed the loss of their primary care centre to wider structural inequalities. Unemployment, poverty, ill health, forced emigration, family breakdown, moral opprobrium and cultural powerlessness resulted in children being taken into state care and subsequently experiencing multiple abuses that impacted negatively on their ability to learn literacy. State care-lessness was therefore causal both in their original disadvantage and their subsequent neglect in the industrial school. In later years, the state's acknowledgement of its neglect of survivors did much to relieve the stigma that is still widely attached to unmet literacy needs. In this case, educational disadvantage was clearly identified as an integral part of the wider package of social harm and inequality that was beyond individual control.

Ongoing state care-lessness

At the same time apologies are not always accompanied by change and there is ample evidence in Ireland and across the globe that literacy continues to function as a barometer for structural inequalities of all kinds. This includes disparities in the concern shown by states for the literacy outcomes of citizens. Depending on the social structures, literacy distribution mirrors class, gender, ethnic and other hierarchies of wealth, status and power (Commission of the European Communities, 2008; OECD, 2009; UNESCO, 2012; Wilkinson and Pickett, 2009). Social groups, locations, schools and entire countries are labelled disadvantaged as if this was a matter of chance rather than the result of political choices. Compensatory programmes to close the literacy gap show scant evidence of redressing learning inequalities (Smyth and McCoy, 2009).

Survivors of abuse in industrial schools were stripped of value and denied the compassion of a just society as described by Nussbaum in her capability theory (Nussbaum, 2001). So too, many other adults today find themselves denied the opportunity to do things:

> In a 'truly human' way, a way informed by an adequate education, including, but by no means limited to, literacy and basic mathematical and scientific training.   (Nussbaum, 2001: 417)

Denied the basic skills for inclusion in the text rich era, adults with unmet literacy needs are likely to earn less, be less active in civic activities or to vote in elections that might encourage more egalitarian policies (Bynner and Parsons, 1997; 2002; Bird and Akerman, 2005). Other political choices can be made by states that invest in more equal structures and accrue more just literacy outcomes. The small Indian state of Kerala is not rich but it is equitable and (at ninety-five percent) has the highest literacy rate of all India (Dorling, 2012).

The state ethic of care in Kerala is evident not just in its concern for literacy but also in its attentiveness to resource, gender, ethnic and religious equality. Kerala demonstrates that even without lavish resources, where there is a vision and a will, things can be done differently.

A learning care chain

Like Freire (1997) in his later text, *Pedagogy of the Heart*, one of the research participants, Bridget, argued for an ideal, inclusive, participative view of the state where interdependency is recognised and acted upon by all. This would link families, schools and colleges, the state and civic society in the learning carer role. Placing limits on those for whom we should have concern meant she and others were pushed to the margins of care. She proposed that our interrelatedness brings with it responsibilities that make us inalienably part of one another and accountable for what happens to our fellow beings. In her analysis, Bridget identifies the links in the chain of care at primary, secondary and tertiary level that are underwritten by the intent and actions of the state and civic society.

> Do you know it might sound simplistic but it is every adult's responsibility to ensure that every child is educated. If we all just look after our own— that is why we were the way we were. Those adults who couldn't look after us were equally abandoned by all the adults who could have helped out but instead abused them every way they could.   *Bridget*

Why lifelong learning care matters

The case for lifelong learning care outlined here matters because literacy inequalities persist and are clearly located in individuals and groups that are treated with less value and importance than others. For literacy practitioners this idea of learning care is significant, not just in providing a new perspective on the social practice context, but also in beginning to identify what learning care means in terms of literacy work.

Those who learned literacy in industrial schools identified continuity of primary care as a decisive factor and family literacy is an immediate way of supporting disadvantaged families in this literacy support role. Even small amounts of primary learning care, for children in industrial schools, was a source of self-esteem, gave some security of identity and afforded the protection of a caring background family presence. Without even small affections, school was tense, unforgiving, and repressive. Low expectations of learners became self-fulfilling as trust was repeatedly betrayed and hopes of learning were paralysed by care-less relationships and impoverished pedagogy.

Secondary learning care in the context of adult literacy suggests a process that delivers on high expectations for all learners through insightful, creative learning relationships grounded in skill and expertise adapted to meet diverse needs. An important aspect of adult literacy learning is the respectful sharing of power between learners and tutors and the enabling of new patterns of power through solidary learning care between peers.

Unequal social contexts are pitted with assumptions about who can and who will learn literacy, whose language merits recognition and reproduction, and what styles of learning are privileged in school and adult learning environments. These issues have affective dimensions that are easily overshadowed by the pervasive imperatives of accreditation, performativity and profit.

This research carried out with survivors of institutional abuse in Irish industrial schools suggests that understanding inequalities in the affective domain may well be pivotal to literacy work. Home is undoubtedly the primary place of care, and secondary care in school and adult learning can be transformational. Nevertheless, the learning care capacity of the family (and the school) is determined, to a great extent, by the state's achievements with regard to creating a more equal society. The state enables or restricts the policies and systems that shape how egalitarian a society is and whether its goods are shared in a fair and just manner (Baker, 1987; Baker *et al.*, 2004). The legislative and policy decisions made by the state, in practice, constitute choices about learning care equality and this is evidently as true today as in the excesses of care-lessness that were experienced in the industrial schools of the past. There may still many learning care lessons to be learned if our education systems are to deliver equality and justice for all learners.

References

Aldridge, F. and Lavender, P. (2000) *The impact of learning on health*, Leicester: National Institute of Adult and Continuing Education.

Allat, P. (1993) Becoming privileged, in Bates, I. and Riseborough, G. (eds.) *Youth and Inequality*, Milton Keynes: Open University Press, 139-159.

Allen, K. (2007) *The corporate takeover of Ireland*, Dublin: Irish Academic Press.

Alvermann, D. (2000) Effective literacy instruction for adolescents, *Journal of Literacy Research*, 34 (2): 189-208.

Anderson, M. (1965) Literacy and schooling on the development threshold: Some historical cases, in Anderson, C.A., and Bowman, M.A. (eds.) *Education and Economic Development*, Chicago: Aldine.

Apple, M. (1993a) Between moral regulation and democracy: The cultural contradictions of the text, in McLaren, P. (ed.) *Critical literacy: Politics, praxis and the postmodern*, State University of New York: Albany, 193-216.

Apple, M. (1993b) *Official knowledge: Democratic education in a conservative age*, New York: Routledge.

Archer, P. & Weir, S. (2005) *Addressing disadvantage: A review of the international literature and of the strategy in Ireland.* Report to the Educational Disadvantage Committee, November 2004, Dublin: Educational Disadvantage Committee.

Aronowitz, S. and Giroux, H. (1993) *Education still under siege*, Massachusetts: Bergin and Garvey.

Askew, S. and Carnell, E. (1998) *Transforming learning: Individual and global change*, London: Casell.

Atkinson, T. (2012) Beyond disempowering counts: Mapping a fruitful future for adult literacies, in Tett, L., Hamilton, M., and Crowther, J., (eds) *More powerful literacies*, Leicester: NIACE.

Bailey, I. and Coleman, U. (1998) *Access and participation in adult literacy schemes*, Dublin: National Adult Literacy Agency.

Baker, J. (1987) *Arguing for equality*, New York: Verso.

Baker, J., Lynch, K., Cantillon, S. and Walsh, J. (2004) *Equality: From theory to action*, London: Palgrave Macmillan.

Baker, J., Lynch, K., Cantillon, S., and Walsh, J. (2009) *Equality: From theory to action, second ed.*, London: Palgrave Macmillan.

Balatti, J., Black, S., and Falk, I. (2006) *Reframing adult literacy and numeracy course outcomes: A social capital perspective*, Adelaide: National Centre for Vocational Education Research (NCVER).

Ball, S. (2003) The teacher's soul and the terrors of performativity, *Journal of Education Policy*, 18 (2): 215-228.

Ball, S. (2010) New class inequalities in education: Why education policy maybe looking in the wrong place! Education policy, civil society and social class, *International Journal of Sociology and Social Policy*, 30 (3/4): 155-166.

Barr, J. (1999) *Liberating knowledge: research, feminism and adult education*, Leicester: NIACE.

Barton, D. (1994) *Literacy: An introduction to the ecology of written language*, Oxford: Blackwell.

Barton, D. (2005) When the magic of literacy wears thin, *Literacy and Numeracy Studies,* 14 (2): 93-97.

Barton, D. (2007) *Literacy: An introduction to the ecology of written language second ed.,* Oxford: Blackwell.

Barton, D. and Hamilton, M. (1998) *Local literacies: Reading and writing in one community,* London: Routledge.

Barton, D., Hamilton, M., and Ivanič, R. (2000) *Situated literacies: Reading and writing in context,* London: Routledge.

Baynham, M. (2006) Agency and contingency in language learning of refugee and asylum seekers, *Linguistics and Education,* 17 (1): 24-39.

Bentley, T. (1998) *Learning beyond the classroom: Education for a changing world,* London: Routledge.

Bird, V. and Akerman, R. (2005) *Every which way we can: A literacy and social inclusion position paper,* London: National Literacy Trust.

Boal, A. (2000) *Theatre of the Oppressed,* London: Pluto.

Bourdieu, P. (1986) The forms of Capital, in Richardson, J., (ed.) *Handbook of Theory and Research for the Sociology of Education,* Connecticut: Greenwood, 214-258.

Bowl, M. and Tobias, R. (2011) Learning from the past, organizing for the future: Adult education in Aotearoa New Zealand, *Adult Education Quarterly,* 62 (3): 272-286.

Brandt, D. and Clinton, T. (2002) Limits of the local: Expanding perspectives on literacy as social practice, *Journal of Literacy Research,* 34 (3): 337-356.

Brewer, J. (2000) *Ethnography,* Milton Keynes: OU.

Brighouse, H. (2003) Educational equality and targeting resources: A pragmatic alternative to the comprehensive ideal, in *Learning and Skills Research* 6 (3): 11-13.

Bubeck, D. (1995) *Care, Justice and Gender,* Oxford: Oxford University Press.

Bynner, J. and Parsons, S. (1997) *It doesn't get any better: The impact of poor basic skills on the lives of 37 year olds,* London: The Basic Skills Agency.

Bynner, J. and Parsons, S. (2002) *Basic skills and social exclusion,* London: The Basic Skills Agency.

Canadian Council on Learning (CCL) (2009) *Why boys don't like to read: Gender differences in reading achievement,* Toronto: CCL.

Carspecken, P. F. (1996) *Critical ethnography in educational research,* London: Routledge.

Carspecken, P. F. and Apple, M. (1992) Critical qualitative research: theory, methodology and practice, in Le Compte, M., Millroy, W. L., and Preissle, J. (eds.) *The Handbook of Qualitative Research in Education,* London: Academic Press: 507-553.

Centre for Educational Research and Innovation (CERI) (1992) *The OECD international education indicators,* Paris: OECD.

Centre for Longitudinal Studies (2010) *Children of the 21st Century: The first five years,* London: CLS.

Chomsky, N. (2000) *Chomsky on miseducation,* Maryland: Rowman and Littlefield.

Chomsky, N. (2001) *Secrets, lies and democracy,* Tucson, Arizona: Odonian Press.

Clancy, P., Drudy, S., Lynch K., and O'Dowd, L. (1995) *Irish society: Sociological perspectives,* Dublin: IPA.

Clancy, P. (2001) *College entry in focus: A fourth national survey of access to higher education,* Dublin: HEA.

Clanchy, M. T. (1979) *From memory to written record: England 1066-1307,* London: Arnold.

Clarke, J. (2002) A new kind of symmetry: Actor—network theories and New Literacy Studies, in *Studies in the Education of Adults,* 34 (2): 107-122, Leicester: NIACE.

Cohen, J. (2006) Social, emotional, ethical and academic education: creating a climate for learning, participation in democracy and well-being, *Harvard Educational Review*, 76 (2): 201–37.

Cohen, L., Manion, L., and Morrison K. (2000) *Research Methods in Education*, London: Routledge.

Coldrey, B. (1993) *The scheme: The Christian Brothers and child care in Western Australia*, O'Connor, Western Australia: Argyle-Pacific.

Commission of the European Communities (CEC) (2001) *Making a European area of lifelong learning a reality*, Brussels: European Commission.

Commission of the European Communities (CEC) (2008) *Progress towards the Lisbon objectives in education and Training: Indicators and benchmarks*, Brussels: DGEAC.

Commission of the European Communities (CEC) (2010) *Strategic Framework for European Cooperation In Education and Training (ET2020)*, Brussels: DGEAC.

Commission to Inquire into Child Abuse (2003) *Third interim report*, Dublin: Stationery Office.

Corridan, M. (2002) *Moving from the Margins*, Dublin: DALC.

Cosgrove, J., Sofroniou, N., Kelly, A., and Shiel, G. (2003) *A teachers'guide to the reading literacy achievements of Irish 15-year olds*, Dublin: ERC.

Cox, W. (2011) *The Impact of NALA's student development work 2007–2010*, Dublin: National Adult Literacy Agency.

Crane Bag (1982) *Peadar Kirby Interview with Paulo Freire*, in *Crane Bag*, Dublin: Crane Bag.

Cregan, A. (2007) From difference to disadvantage: 'Talking posh'. Sociolinguistic perspectives on the context of schooling in Ireland, Research Working Paper 07/03, Dublin: Poverty Research Institute/Combat Poverty Agency.

Cressy, D. (1977) *Literacy and the Social Order: Reading and Writing in Tudor and Stuart England*, Cambridge—New York: Cambridge University Press.

Crowther, J., Hamilton, M., and Tett, L. (2001) *Powerful Literacies*, Leicester: NIACE.

Daly, M., and Leonard, M. (2002) *Against all the odds: Family life on a low income in Ireland*, Dublin: IPA and CPA.

Darmanin, M. (2003) When students are failed: 'love' as an alternative education discourse? *International Studies in Sociology of Education*, 13, (2): 141-170.

Dasgupta, P.S. (1995) *An inquiry into well-being and destitution*, Oxford: Oxford University Press.

Deegan, J., Devine, D. and Lodge, A. (2004) *Primary Voices*, Dublin: IPA.

Denny, K. (2002) New methods for comparing literacy across populations: insights from the measurement of poverty, *Journal of the Royal Statistical Society: Series A (Statistics in Society)* 165 (3): 481–493.

Denny, K., Harmon, C., McMahon, D. and Redmond, S. (1999) Analysis of the International Adult Literacy Survey for Ireland, *The Economic and Social Review*, 30 (3): 215-226.

Denzin, N. K. (1997) Triangulation in educational research in Keeves, J.P. (ed.) *Educational research, methodology and measurement: An international handbook*, Oxford: Elsevier Science, 318-22.

Department of Education for Northern Ireland, (1998) *Compendium of NI education statistics*, Belfast: DENI.

Department of Education and Science, (2000) *Learning for life: White paper on adult education*, Dublin: Stationery Office.

Department of Education and Science, (2002) *Towards redress and recovery: Report by the Compensation Advisory Committee, January 2002,* Dublin: Government Publications.

Department of Education and Science, (2005) *Literacy and numeracy in disadvantaged schools: Challenges for teachers and learners,* Dublin: Government Publications.

Department of Education and Science (2006) *Joint committee on education and science: Adult literacy in Ireland,* Dublin: Government Publications.

Dohan, D. and Sanchez-Jankowski M. (1998) Using computers to analyse ethnographic field data: Theoretical and practical considerations, *Annual Review of Sociology,* 465-486.

Dorling, D. (2004) Prime suspect: Murder in Britain, in Hillyard, P., Pantazis, C., Tombs, S. and Gordon, D. (eds.) *Beyond criminology: Taking harm seriously,* London: Pluto. 178-192.

Dorling, D. (2012) *The no nonsense guide to equality,* Oxford: New Internationalist.

Doyle, P. (1988) *The God Squad,* Dublin: Raven's Art Press.

Duru-Bellat, M. (2008) Recent trends in social reproduction in France: should the political promises of education be revisited? *Journal of Education Policy,* 23 (1): 81-95.

Duncan, W. (1993) The constitutional protection of parental rights, in Eekelaar, J.M. and Sarcevic, P. (eds.) *Parenthood in modern society: Legal and social issues for the twenty first century,* Dordrecht: Martinus Nijhoff.

DuVivier, E. (1991) How many illiterates? Towards an estimate of the incidence of reading and writing difficulties among Irish adults, *Studies in Education,* 7, 7-28.

Eady, M. J., Herrington, A. J. and Jones S. C. (2010) Literacy practitioners' perspectives on adult learning needs and technology approaches in indigenous communities, *Australian Journal of Adult Learning* 50 (2): 260-286.

Edmondson, R. (2000) Writing between worlds, in Byrne, A. and Lentin, R. (eds.) *(Re) searching women: Feminist research methodologies in the social sciences in Ireland,* Dublin: IPA.

Educational Research Centre (2004) *Reading literacy in disadvantaged schools,* Dublin: ERC.

Eisenstein, E. (1968) Some conjectures about the impact of printing on western society and thought: A preliminary report, *Journal of Modern History,* 40 (1): 1-56.

Eivers, E., Shiel, G., Perkins, R. and Cosgrove, J. (2005) *Succeeding in reading? Reading standards in Irish primary schools,* Dublin: Stationery Office.

English, E., Hargreaves L. and Hislam, J. (2002) Pedagogical dilemmas in the National Literacy Strategy: primary teachers' perceptions, reflections and classroom behaviour, *Cambridge Journal of Education,* 32 (1): 9-26.

Engster, D. (2004) Care ethics and natural law theory: Toward and institutional political theory of caring, *The Journal of Politics,* 66 (1): 113-135.

Engster, D. (2005) Rethinking care theory: the practice of caring and the obligation to care, *Hypatia,* 20 (3): 50–74.

Engster, D. (2007) *The heart of justice: Care ethics and political theory,* Oxford: Oxford University Press.

Fahey, T. (2007) The case for an EU-wide measure of poverty, *European Sociological Review* 23 (1): 35-47.

Fahy, B. (1999) *Freedom of angels: Surviving Goldenbridge orphanage.* Dublin: O'Brien Press.

Fawns, M. and Ivanic, R. (2001) Form-filling as a social practice: Taking power into our own hands, in Crowther, J., Hamilton, M. and Tett, L. (eds.) *Powerful Literacies,* Leicester: NIACE.

Fecho, B. (2001) Why are you doing this? Acknowledging and transcending threat in critical inquiry classrooms, *Research in the teaching of english*, 36 (1): 9-37.

Feeley, M. (2001) *Unlocking potential*, Belfast: Basic Skills Unit.

Feeley, M. (2005) *Exploring an egalitarian theory of adult literacy*, http://education-line@ leeds.ac.uk.

Feeley, M. (2007) Redefining Literacy from an Egalitarian Perspective, *The Adult Learner*, Dublin: AONTAS. 13-25.

Feeley, M. (2009) Living in care and without love: the impact of affective inequalities on learning literacy, in *Affective equality: Who cares?* (eds.) Lynch, K., Baker, J. and Lyons, M., London: Palgrave. 199-216.

Feeley, M. (2010) Literacy learning care: exploring the role of care in literacy learning with survivors of abuse in Irish industrial schools, *The Adult Learner* Dublin: AONTAS, 72–90.

Feeley, M. (2012) Affective power: Exploring the concept of *learning care* in the context of adult literacy, in Tett, L., Hamilton, M., and Crowther, J. (eds) *More powerful literacies*, Leicester: NIACE.131-147.

Feinstein, L., Hammond, C., Woods, L., Preston, J. and Bynner, J. (2003) *The contribution of adult learning to health and social capital*, London: Institute of Education.

Field, J. (2000) *Lifelong learning and the New Educational Order*, London: Trentham.

Field, J. (2002) *Promoting European dimensions in lifelong learning*, Leicester: NIACE.

Fine, G. and Smith, G. (2000) *Erving Goffman*, London: Sage.

Fineman, M. (2004) *The autonomy myth: A theory of dependency*, New York: New Press.

Florio-Ruane, S. and McVee, M. (2000) Ethnographic approaches to literacy education, in Kamil, M. L., Mosenthal, P.B., Pearson, P.D. and Barr, R. (eds.) *Handbook of Reading Research 3*, New Jersey: Lawrence Erlbaum Associates.

Flynn, M. (2003) *Nothing to Say*, Dublin: Lilliput Press.

Flynn, M. (2003a) *James X*, Dublin: Lilliput Press.

Fowler, E. and Mace, J. (2005) *Outside the classroom: Researching literacy with adult learners*, Leicester: NIACE.

Foucault, M. (1975) *Discipline and punish: The birth of the prison*, New York: Pantheon.

Freire, P. (1972) *Pedagogy of the oppressed*, London: Penguin.

Freire, P. (1973) *Education for critical consciousness*, New York: Continuum.

Freire, P. (1996) *Pedagogy of hope*, New York: Continuum.

Freire, P. (1997) *Pedagogy of the heart*, New York: Continuum.

Freire, P. (2001) *Pedagogy of freedom: Ethics, democracy and civic courage*, New York: Rowman and Littlefield.

Freire, P. and Macedo, D. (1987) *Reading the word and the world*, London: Routledge.

Gabriel, C. (2006) Training the excluded for work: Access and equity for women, immigrants, First Nations, youth, and people with low income, *Canadian Journal of Political Science*, 39, 187-189.

Gannerud, E. (2001) A gender perspective on the work and lives of women primary school teachers, *Scandinavian Journal of Educational Research*, 45 (1): 55–70.

Gardner, H. (1993) *Multiple Intelligences: The theory in practice*, New York: Basic Books.

Gardner, Howard (1999) *Intelligence reframed: Multiple Intelligences for the 21st Century*, NY: Basic Books.

Gee, J.P. (1999) The New Literacy Studies: from 'socially situated' to the work of the social, in Barton, D., Hamilton, M. and Ivanic, R. (eds.) *Situated Literacies*, London: Routledge.

Gheaus, A. (2009) How much of what matters can we redistribute? Love, justice and luck, *Hypatia* 24 (4): 63-83.

Gheaus, A. (2013) Care drain: who should provide for the children left behind? *Critical Review of International Social and Political Philosophy,* 16 (1): 1-23.

Giddens, A. (1994) *Beyond left and right: The future of radical politics*, Oxford: Polity.

Giroux, H. (1987) Literacy and the pedagogy of political empowerment, Introduction to *Literacy: Reading the Word and the World*, Freire, P. and Macedo, D. (eds.) London: Routledge.

Goffman, E. (1961) Asylums: essays on the social situation of mental patients and other inmates, New York: Anchor Books.

Goffman, E. (1963) *Stigma: Notes on the management of spoiled identity*, Englewood Cliffs, New Jersey: Prentice-Hall.

Goldberg, S. (2000) *Attachment and development*, London: Arnold.

Golding, B., Brown, M., Foley, A., Harvey, J. and Gleeson, L. (2007) *Men's sheds in Australia: Learning through community contexts*, Adelaide: National Centre for Vocational Education Research (NCVER).

Goleman, D. (1996) *Emotional intelligence*, New York: Bantam Books.

Government of Ireland (1970) *Reformatory and industrial schools in Ireland* (Prl. 1342, Kennedy Report), Dublin: Government Publication.

Graff, H. J. (1981) *Literacy and social development in the West*, New York: Cambridge University Press.

Gramsci, A. (1971) *Selections from prison notebooks*, London: Lawrence and Wishart.

Gramsci, A. (1995) *Further selections from the prison notebooks* (ed. and tr.) Boothman, D., London: Lawrence and Wishart.

Graycar, R. and Wangmann, J. (2007) Redress packages for institutional child abuse: Exploring the Grandview Agreement as a case study in *'Alternative' Dispute Resolution*, Sydney Law School, Research Paper No. 07/50.

Green, S. (2003) Involving fathers in family literacy, *Family Literacy Forum and Literacy Harvest (Fall)*, New York: Literacy Assistance Centre.

Gregory, E. and Williams, A. (2004) Living literacies in homes and communities, in Grainger, T. (ed.) *The Routledge Falmer Reader in Language and Literacy*, London: Routledge. 33-51.

Gross, R. (2001) *Psychology: The science of the mind and behaviour*, London: Hodder and Stoughton.

Habermas, J. (1984) *Reason and the rationalization of society,* Volume 1 of *The Theory of Communicative Action*, tr. McCarthy, T., Boston: Beacon Press.

Hackett, C. (2004) Narratives of political activism from women in West Belfast, in Ward, M. and Ryan, L. (eds) *Irish women and nationalism: soldiers, new women and wicked hags,* Dublin: Irish Academic Press.

Hackett, C. (2006) Recording oral history: Practical and ethical issues, in McGowan, J. (ed.) *Hear and now and then part three: A report from the discussion forum for researchers*, Belfast: Community Relations Council.

Hamilton, M. (1998) Histories and horoscopes: The ethnographer as fortuneteller, *Anthropology and Education Quarterly* 29 (3): 1-10.

Hamilton, M. (2000) Sustainable literacies and the ecology of lifelong Learning, Paper presented at *Supporting Lifelong Learning: A Global Colloquium*, London, England, July 5-7, 2000.

Hamilton, M. and Barton, D. (2000) The International Adult Literacy Survey: What does it really measure? *International Journal of Education* 46 (5): 377–89. Hamburg: UNESCO.

Hamilton, M. and Hillier, Y. (2006) *The changing face of adult literacy, language and numeracy 1970-2000: A critical history*, Stoke-on-Trent: Trentham Books.

Hammersley, M. (1995) *The politics of social research*, London: Sage.

Hammersley, M. and Atkinson, P. (1994) *Handbook of qualitative research*, London: Sage.

Hannan, D. and Shortall, S. (1991) *The quality of their education: School leavers' views of educational objectives and outcomes*, Dublin: Economic and Social Research Institute (ESRI).

Hargreaves, A. (2000) Mixed emotions: teachers' perceptions of their interactions with students, *Teaching and Teacher Education*, 16 (8): 811–26.

Hargreaves, A. (2001) Emotional geographies of teaching, *Teachers' College Record*, 103 (6): 1056–80.

Harmon, C. and Walker, I. (2003) Education and earnings in Europe, *Economics of Education Review*, 22 (4): 445-446.

Health Board Executive (HBE) (2002) *The National Counselling Service, first report*, Dublin: Health Boards Executive.

Healy, S. and Reynolds, B. (1999) Towards a new vision of social partnership: Values, content, process and structure' in Healy, S. and Reynolds, B. (eds.) *Social Partnership in a New Century*, Dublin: CORI.

Heath, S. B. (1983) *Ways with words: Language, life and work in communities and classrooms*, New York: Cambridge University Press.

Heckman, J., and Masterov, D. (2004) The productivity argument for investing in young children, Working Paper No 5, Washington DC: Committee on Economic Development.

Hegarty, A. and Feeley, M. (2009) *Literacy-friendly further education and training*. Dublin: NALA.

Hegarty, A. and Feeley, M. (2010) *Taking care of family literacy work: An enquiry with parents about their experience of nurturing language and literacy in the home*, Dublin: NALA.

Herman, J. (1997) *Trauma and recovery*, New York: Basic Books.

Hillyard, P., Kelly, G., McLaughlin, E. and Tomlinson, M. (2003) *Bare necessities: Poverty and social exclusion in Northern Ireland*, Belfast: Democratic Dialogue.

Hillyard, P., Pantazis, C., Tombs, S. and Gordon, D. (2004) *Beyond criminology—Taking harm seriously*, London: Pluto.

Hodge, R. (2003) *A review of recent ethnographies of literacy*, Lancaster Literacy Research Centre Working Papers Series, No 1.

Hogg, M and G. Vaughan (1998) *Social Psychology*, UK: Prentice Hall.

hooks, bell (1989) *Talking back: Thinking feminist, thinking black*, Boston, Massachusetts: South End Press.

hooks, bell (1990) *Yearning: race, gender and cultural politics*, Toronto: Between the Lines.

hooks, bell (1994) *Teaching to transgress: Education as the practice of freedom*, New York: Routledge.

hooks, bell (1997) Homeplace: A site of resistance, in McDowell, L. (ed.) *Undoing place? A geographical reader*, New York: Arnold. (33-38).

hooks, bell (2000) *Feminist theory: From margin to centre*, London: Pluto.

hooks, bell (2003) *Teaching community: A pedagogy of hope*, New York: Routledge.

Horsman, J. (2000) *Moving forward: Approaches and activities to support women's learning*, Toronto: Parkdale Project Read.

Horsman, J. (2004) But is it education? The challenge of creating effective learning for survivors of trauma, *Women's Studies Quarterly*, Special Issue on Women and Literacy, Toronto: Parkdale Project Read.

Horsman, J. and Norton, M. (1999) A framework to encourage and support practitioner involvement in adult literacy research in practice in Canada, A paper prepared for the National Literacy Secretariat.

Inglis, T. (1998) *Moral monopoly: The rise and fall of the Catholic church in modern Ireland, second ed.* Dublin: University College Dublin Press.

Instituto del Terco Mundo (2003) *World Guide 2003/2004,* Oxford: New Internationalist.

Jackson, B. (1964) *Streaming: an education system in miniature*, London: Routledge.

Jeffrey, B. and Walford, G. (2004) *Ethnographies of educational and cultural conflicts: Strategies and resolutions*, London: Elsevier.

Kellaghan, T., Weir, S., O'hUallachain, S. and Morgan, M. (1995) *Educational disadvantage in Ireland,* Dublin: Education Research Centre.

Kim, J. (2003) Challenges to NLS: Response to 'What's new in New Literacy Studies', *Current Issues in Comparative Education*, 5 (2): 119-121.

Kittay, E. (2002) Love's labor revisited, *Hypatia* 17 (3): 237-250.

Kress, G. (2010) *Multimodality: a social semiotic approach to contemporary communication*, London: Routledge.

Kress, G. and Van Leeuwen, T. (1996) *Reading images—The grammar of visual design*, London: Routledge.

Kress, G. and Street, B. (2006) Multi-modality and literacy practices, foreword to *Travel notes from the New Literacy Studies: Case studies of practice*, in Pahl, K. and Rosewell, J. (eds.) Bristol: Multilingual Matters Ltd.

Lankshear, C. (1997) *Changing Literacies*, Milton Keynes: OU.

Lankshear, C. and Knobel, M. (2003) *New literacies: Changing knowledge and classroom learning*, Milton Keynes: OU.

Lather, P. (1991) *Getting smart: Feminist research and pedagogy with /in the postmodern*, New York: Routledge.

Laughlin, J., & Leman, D. (2010) Redefining success in aboriginal learning in Canada, Ottawa, Ontario, Canada: Canadian Council on Learning (CCL).

Lee, V. and Burkham, D. (2002) *Inequality at the starting gate: Social background differences in achievement as children begin school*, Washington DC: Economic Policy Institute.

Lemert, C. and Branaman, A. (1997) *The Goffman Reader*, Massachusetts: Blackwell Publishers.

Le Roy Ladurie, E. (1977) *The peasants of Languedoc*, tr. John Day, Urbana: University of Illinois Press.

Le Roy Ladurie, E. (1978) *Montaillou: Cathars and Catholics in a French village, 1294-1324*, London: Scholar Press.

Literacy Assistance Centre (2003) Family literacy forum and Literacy Harvest (Fall), New York: Literacy Assistance Centre.

Lorde, A. (1984) *Sister outsider: Essays and speeches*, New York: Crossing Press.

Luttrell, W. (2013) Children's counter-narratives of care, in Special Issue (ed.) Devine, D. and Luttrell, W., The 'valuing' of children in education in neo-liberal times—global perspectives; local practices, *Children and Society* 27 (4) (forthcoming July 2013).

Lynch, K. (1989) Solidary labour: Its nature and marginalisation, *Sociological Review* 37, 1-14.

Lynch, K. (1999) *Equality in Education*, Dublin: Gill and Macmillan.

Lynch, K. (2007) Love labour as a distinct and non-commodifiable form of care labour, *The Sociological Review*, 55 (3): 550–70.

Lynch, K. and Baker, J. (2005) Equality in education: an equality of condition perspective, *Theory and Research in Education*, 3 (2) 131–64.

Lynch, K. and Feeley, M. (2009) *Gender and education (and employment): Gendered imperatives and their implications for women and men—lessons from research for policy makers*. NESSE: DGEAC.

Lynch, K. and Lodge, A. (2002) *Equality and power in schools: Redistribution, recognition and representation*, London: Routledge.

Lynch, K. and McLaughlin, E. (1995) Caring labour and love labour, in Clancy, P., Drudy, S., Lynch, K. and O'Dowd, L. (eds.) *Irish Society: Sociological Perspectives*, Dublin: IPA, 250-92.

Lynch, K. and Moran, M. (2006) Markets, schools and the convertibility of economic capital: the complex dynamics of class choice, *British Journal of Sociology of Education*, 27 (2): 221-235.

Lynch, K. and O'Neill, C. (1994) The colonisation of social class in education, *British Journal of Sociology in Education*, 15, 307-324.

Lynch, K., Baker, J. and Lyons, M. (eds.) (2009) *Affective equality: Love, care and injustice*, London: Palgrave.

Lynch, K., Lyons, M. and Cantillon, S. (2007) Breaking silence: educating citizens for love, care and solidarity, *International Studies in Sociology of Education*, 7 (1–2) 1–19.

Lyons, M., Lynch, K., Close, S., Sheerin, E. and Boland, P. (2003) *Inside classrooms: the teaching and learning of mathematics in social context*, Dublin: IPA.

Mace, J. (1995) *Literacy, language and community publishing: Essays in adult education*, Clevedon: Multilingual Matters.

Mace, J. (1998) *Playing with time: Mothers and the meaning of literacy*, London: Taylor and Francis.

Mace, J. (2001) Signatures and the lettered world, in Crowther, J., Hamilton, M. and Tett, L. (eds.) *Powerful literacies*, Leicester: NIACE.

Machin, S. (2006) Social disadvantage and educational experiences, OECD Social, Employment and Migration Working Papers: No 32.

McCaffrey, J. (2009) Gypsies and travellers: Literacy, discourse and communication practices, *Compare*, 39 (5): 643-657.

McClave, H. (2005) *Education for citizenship: A capabilities approach*. Unpublished PhD thesis, UCD Equality Studies Centre, University College Dublin.

McGivney, V. (2001) *Fixing or changing the pattern*, Leicester: NIACE.

McMinn, J. (2000) *The changers and the changed*, Unpublished PhD Thesis, Equality Studies Centre, University College Dublin.

MacRuairc, G. (2004) 'Big mad words'—Schools, social class and children's perceptions of language variation, in Deegan, J., Devine, D. and Lodge, A. (eds.) *Primary voices: Equality, diversity and childhood in Irish primary schools*, Dublin: IPA.

Morgan, M., Hickey B. and Kellaghan T. (1997) *IALS: Results for Ireland*, Dublin: Government Publications.

Morgan, M., and Kett, M. (2003) *The prison adult literacy survey*, Dublin: Department of Justice and Law Reform.

Moser, C. (1999) *A fresh start: Improving literacy and numeracy*, London: DfEE.

National Adult Literacy Agency (NALA) (2004) *Working together: Approaches to family literacy*, Dublin: NALA.

National Adult Literacy Agency (2011) *Providing leadership in adult literacy: Strategic plan 2011–2013*. Dublin: NALA.

National Adult Literacy Agency (2012) *NALA factsheet: Participation in the VEC Adult Literacy Service 2011*, Dublin: NALA.

National Anti-Poverty Strategy (NAPS) (1997) *Sharing in progress*, Dublin: Stationery Office.

National Anti-Poverty Strategy Review (2002) *Building an inclusive society,* Dublin: Stationery Office.

National Economic and Social Forum (NESF) (2009) *Child literacy and social inclusion: Implementation issues*, Dublin: NESDO.

Northern Ireland Civic Forum (NICF) (2002) *Can do better: Educational disadvantage in the context of lifelong learning*, Belfast: NICF.

National Research and Development Council (NRDC) (2005) *Embedded teaching and learning of adult literacy, numeracy and ESOL: Seven case studies of embedded provision*, London: NRDC.

Noddings, N. (1992) *The Challenge to care in schools: An alternative approach to education.* New York: Teachers' College Press.

Noddings, N. (2006) Educating whole people: a response to Jonathan Cohen, *Harvard Educational Review*, 76 (2): 238–42.

Noddings, N. (2007) *Philosophy of education*, second ed. Boulder, Colorado: Westview Press.

Nussbaum, M. (2000) *Women and human development*, New York: Cambridge.

Nussbaum, M. (2001) *Upheavals of thought: The intelligence of emotions*, New York: Cambridge.

Oates, M.J. (1995) *The Catholic philanthropic tradition in America.* Bloomington: Indiana University Press.

O'Brien, M. (2005) Mothers as educational workers: mothers' emotional work at their children's transfer to second-level education, *Irish Educational Studies*, 24 (2–3) 223–42.

O'Brien, M. (2007) Mothers' emotional care work in education and its moral imperative, *Gender and Education*, 19 (2): 159–57.

O'Brien, M. (2008) *Well-being and post primary schooling: A review of the literature and research*, Dublin: NCCA.

O'Brien, M. (2011) Towards a pedagogy of care and well-being, in (eds.) O'Shea, A. and O'Brien, M., *Pedagogy, oppression and transformation in a 'post-critical' climate*, London: Continuum. 14-36.

OECD (1992) *Education at a glance: OECD indicators, 1991*, Paris: OECD.

OECD (1995) *Literacy, economy and society: Results of the first international adult literacy survey*, Paris: OECD.

OECD, (1996) *The knowledge based economy,* Paris: OECD.

OECD (1997) *Literacy skills for the knowledge society*, Paris: OECD.

OECD (1998) *International adult literacy survey*, Paris: OECD.

OECD (2000) *Literacy in the information age: Final report of the International Adult literacy Survey*, Paris: OECD.

OECD (2006) *Adult literacy and lifeskills survey (ALL)*, Paris: OECD.

OECD (2009) *OECD Programme for International Student Assessment (PISA)*, Paris: OECD.

OECD (2010) *The OECD Programme for the International Assessment of Adult Competencies (PIAAC)*, Paris: OECD.

OECD (2011) *OECD Programme for International Student Assessment (PISA)*, Paris: OECD.

OECD/Statistics Canada (2005) *First results of the adult literacy and life skills survey (ALL)*, Paris/Ottowa: OECD.

Olick, J. K. and Robbins J. (1998) Social Memory Studies: From 'collective memory' to the historical sociology of mnemonic practices, *Annual Review of Sociology*, 24: 105-140.

O'Neill, C. (1992) *Telling it like it is*, Dublin: Combat Poverty Agency.

O'Neill, C. (2000) Naming our own world: Making a case for femininst research,' in Byrne, A., and Lentin, R. (eds.) *(Re)searching women: Feminist research methodologies in the social sciences in Ireland*, Dublin: IPA. 105-118.

O'Reilly, K. (2009) *Key concepts in ethnography*, London: SAGE.

O'Toole, F. (2003) *After the Ball*, Dublin: New Island Press.

Owens, T. (2000) *Men on the move*, Dublin: AONTAS.

Parker, R. (2004) Children and the concept of harm, in Hillyard, P., Pantazis, C., Tombs, S. and Gordon, D. (eds.) *Beyond criminology: Taking harm seriously*, London: Pluto. 236-251.

Parsons and Bynner, (2002) *Basic skills and social exclusion: Findings from a study of adults born in 1970*, London: Basic Skills Agency.

Patton, M. Q. (1980) *Qualitative evaluation methods*, Thousand Oaks, California: Sage.

Patton, M. Q. (1990) *Qualitative evaluation and research methods*, Thousand Oaks, California: Sage.

Payne, R. (2001) Lifelong learning: A national trade union strategy in a global economy, *International Journal of Lifelong Education* 20 (5): 378-392.

Peyroux, C. (1998) Lands of women? Writing the history of early medieval women in Ireland and Europe, in *Early Medieval Europe 7* (2): 217-227.

Phillips, A. (1999) *Which equalities matter?* Cambridge: Polity Press.

Piliavin, J.A, J. Dovidio, S. Gaertner and R. Clark, (1981) *Emergency Intervention*, New York: Academic Press.

Powell, R. (1999) *Literacy as a moral imperative: Facing the challenges of a pluralistic society*, Maryland: Rowman and Littlefield.

Power, Eileen (1995) *Medieval Women*, UK: Cambridge University Press.

Raftery, M. and O'Sullivan E. (1999) *Suffer little children: The inside story of Ireland's industrial schools*, Dublin: New Island.

Reay, D. (1998) *Classwork: Mothers' involvement with their children's primary schooling*, London: UCL Press.

Reay, D. (2000) A useful extension of Bourdieu's conceptual framework?: emotional capital as a way of understanding mothers' involvement in their children's education?, *The Sociological Review*, 48 (4): 568–85.

Reay, D., Crozier, G. and Clayton, J. (2010) 'Fitting in' and 'standing out': working–class students in UK higher education, *British Educational Research Journal*, 32 (1) 1—19.

Reder, S. and Davila E. (2005) Context and literacy practices, *Annual Review of Applied Linguistics*, 25, 170-187.

Residential Institutions Redress Board (RIRB) (2002) *Residential institutions redress board guidelines*, www.rirb.ie.

Residential Institutions Redress Board (RIRB) (2004) *Residential institutions redress board guidelines*, second ed., www.rirb.ie.

Rogers, A. (2005) Literacy and productive skills training: Embedded literacies, in *Adult Education 65,* online journal available at: http://www.eaea.org/doc/dvv/65. pdf#page=57, accessed 23 February 2009.

Russell, L. (2011) *Understanding pupil resistance: Integrating gender, ethnicity and class,* Stroud: Ethnography and Education Series, Tufnell Press.

Ryan, S. (2009) Commission to inquire into child abuse report (Volumes I—V), Dublin: Stationery Office.

Sacks, D. (2003) *The Alphabet: Unravelling the mystery of the alphabet from A to Z,* London: Huntchinson.

Salmi, J. (2004) Violence in democratic societies: towards an analytic framework, in Hillyard, P., Pantazis, C., Tombs, S. and Gordon, D. (eds.) *Beyond criminology: Taking harm seriously,* London: Pluto. 55-67.

Schofield, R. S. (1973) Dimensions of literacy 1750-1850, in *Explorations in Economic History* 10: 437—454.

Searle, C. (1975) *Classrooms of resistance,* London: Writers' and Readers' Publishing Cooperative.

Searle, C. (1998) *None but our words: Critical literacy in classroom and community,* Milton Keynes: OU.

Sennet, R. (2003) *Respect: The formation of character in a world of inequality,* London: Penguin.

Shelley, S. (2005) Useful outcomes for workers in trade union learning activities: The significance of attitude and ownership. University of Hertfordshire, Business School Working Paper 5.

Shiel, G., Cosgrove, J., Sofroniou, N. and Kelly, A. (2001) *Ready for life? The literacy achievements of Irish 15-year olds with comparative international data,* Dublin: ERC.

Shield, P. (2006) Forty-Seven, today you are nine': Systematic abuse in Irish childcare institutions, in *Group Analysis,* 39 (1): 25-35.

Smythe, S. and Isserlis, J. (2003) The good mother: Exploring mothering discourses in family literacy texts, in *Family Literacy Forum* 2 (2): 25-33.

Smyth, E. and McCoy, S. (2009) *Investing in education: Combating educational disadvantage,* Dublin: ESRI.

Spufford, M. (1979) First steps in literacy: the reading and writing experience of the humblest C17 spiritual autobiographies, *Social History,* 4: 407-435.

Standing, K. (1999) Negotiating the home and the school: Low income and lone mothering and unpaid schoolwork, in McKie, L., Bowlby S. and Gregory, S. (eds.) *Gender, power and the household,* London: Palgrave.

Stevenson, J. (1990) Literacy in Ireland: the evidence of the Patrick dossier in the Book of Armagh, in McKitterick R. (ed.) *The Uses of Literacy in Medieval Europe,* Cambridge: Cambridge University Press, 11-35.

Sticht, T.G. (1999) *Adult Basic Education: Strategies to increase returns on investment (ROI),* El Cajun, California: Applied Behavioural and Cognitive Sciences.

Sticht, T.G. (2000) *Using telephone and mail surveys as a supplement or alternative to door-to-door surveys in the assessment of adult literacy,* Washington DC: National Center for Education Statistics.

Sticht, T. G. (2003) Functional Context Education (FCE) part 1: New interest in FCE theory and principles for integrating basic skills and work skills, http://education.independent. co.uk/further/story.jsp?story=449220.

Sticht, T.G. (2007) Integrated literacy works! Making workforce development efficient and effective in industrialized nations, www.nald.ca/library/research/sticht/07feb/1.htm.

Street, B. (1999) New Literacies in theory and practice: what are the implications for language in education?, *Linguistics in Education,* 10 (1): 1-24.

Street, B. (2001) *Literacy and development: Ethnographic perspectives,* New York: Routledge.

Street, B. (2003) What's 'new' in New Literacy Studies? Critical approaches to literacy in theory and practice, *Current Issues in Comparative Education,* 5 (2): 77-91.

Street, B. (2011) NLS1 and NLS2: Implications of a social literacies perspective for policies and practices of literacy education, in Goodwyn, A. (ed.) *The great literacy debate: A critical response to the Literacy Strategy and Framework for English,* London: Routledge.

Street, B. (2012) Contexts for literacy work: New Literacy Studies, multimodality, and the 'local and the global', in Tett, L., Hamilton, M., and Crowther, J., (eds.) *More powerful literacies,* Leicester: NIACE.

Street, B. and Lefstein, A. (2007) *Literacy: An Advanced Resource Book for Students,* London: Routledge.

Stuart, M. and Thompson A. (1995) Engaging with difference: Education and 'other' adults', in Stuart M. and Thompson A. (eds.) *Engaging with difference: The 'other' in adult education,* Leicester: NIACE.

Taylor, D. (1983) *Family literacy: Young children learning to read and write,* Portsmouth, New Hampshire: Heinemann.

Tett, L., Hamilton, M. and Crowther, J. (2012) *More powerful literacies,* Leicester: NIACE.

Tilly, C. (1999) *Durable Inequalities,* Berkeley, California: University of California Press.

Tusting, K. (2003) The new literacy studies and time: an exploration, in Barton, D., Hamilton, M. and Ivanič, R. (eds.) *Situated literacies,* London: Routledge.

Tyrell, P. (2006) *Founded on fear,* Dublin: Irish Academic Press.

United Nations Development Programme (UNDP) (2002) *Human Development Report 2002: Deepening Democracy in a Fragmented World,* NY: Oxford University.

UNESCO (2006) *Education for all: Literacy for life.* Paris: UNESCO.

UNESCO (2012) *Adult and youth literacy: UIS Report 20,* Paris: UNESCO.

Van Galen, J. (2004) School reform and class work: Teachers as mediators of social class, *Journal of Educational Change,* 5 (2): 111-139.

Ward, J. and Edwards, J. (2002) *Learning journeys: Learners voices. Learners views on progress and achievement in literacy and numeracy,* London: Learning and Skills Development Agency.

Ward, M. (1983) *Unmanageable revolutionaries: Women and Irish nationalism,* London: Pluto.

Ward, T. (2002) *Asylum seekers in adult education: A study of language and literacy needs,* Dublin: CDVEC.

Ward, T. (2004) State harms, in Hillyard, P., Pantazis, C., Tombs, S. and Gordon, D. (eds.) *Beyond criminology: Taking harm seriously,* London: Pluto, (84-101).

Weiler, K. (1988) *Women teaching for change: gender, class and power,* Massachusetts: Bergin and Garvey.

Weiler, K. (1991) Freire and a feminist pedagogy of difference, *Harvard Educational Review,* 61 (4): 449-474.

Wickert, R. and McGuirk, J. (2005) *Integrating literacies: Using partnerships to build literacy capabilities in communities,* Adelaide: NCVER.

Wilkinson, R. (2005) *The impact of inequality: How to make sick societies healthier,* New York: New Press.

Wilkinson, R. and Pickett, K. (2009) *The spirit level: Why more equal societies almost always do better,* London: Allen Lane.

Wise, M. and Signal, L. (2000) Health promotion development in Australia and New Zealand, *Health Promotion International,* 15 (3): 237-248.

Zappone, K. (2003) *Rethinking identity: The challenge of diversity,* Ireland: The joint Equality and Human Rights Forum.

Zaviršek, D. (2006), Ethnographic research as the source of critical knowledge in social work and other caring professions, in Flaker, V., Schmid, T., (eds.) *Von der Idee zur Forschungsarbeit: Forschen in Sozialarbeit un Sozialwissenschaft,* (Böhlau Studienbücher BSB). Wien: Böhlau Verlag, Herbst, 125-144.

Zembylas, M. and Bekerman, Z. (2008) Education and the dangerous memories of historical trauma: narratives of pain, narratives of hope, *Curriculum Inquiry,* 38 (2): 125-154.

Lightning Source UK Ltd.
Milton Keynes UK
UKOW04f1342110314

227926UK00001B/1/P